M000082062

"A thought-provoking, inspiring journey and an important and welcome addition to the world of self-help books."

—New York Journal of Books

"Turn to any page and you will find wisdom to guide you through the joys and sorrows of daily life. I keep this book on my bedside table and read a page every night. Wonderful!"

—Katherine Ketcham, coauthor of *The Spirituality of Imperfection* and *Experiencing Spirituality*

"Kingsley Gallup is passionate about both her personal and professional life, and that translates into offering you an empowering daily journey that allows you to get in touch with your vitality and authenticity. *Project Personal Freedom* is composed of 365 poignant messages, written with respect for its readers, meeting them where they are in their life path. Find your favorites, embrace them, and enjoy life!"

—Claudia Black, PhD, author of *It Will Never Happen to Me* and *The Truth Begins with You*

"Kingsley Gallup's *Project Personal Freedom* is a gem. Beautifully written, it gives us all a blueprint for living a fuller life—our own life."

—Dr. Saul Cooperman, former New Jersey commissioner of education and author of *How Schools Really Work* and *Eddie and Me*

"This book will enable others to live their lives authentically and with great joy. A splendid offering."

PROJECT PERSONAL FREEDOM

PROJECT PERSONAL FREEDOM

tips and tools for a liberated life

KINGSLEY GALLUP, MA, LPC, NCC, DCC

GOODMAN BECK PUBLISHING

PO Box 253
Norwood, NJ 07648
goodmanbeck.com

ISBN 978-1-936636-12-9

Library of Congress Control Number: 2014931453

Printed in the United States of America

10 9 8 7 6 5 4 3 2 1

For my Doodlebug and Lightfoot,

This is my hope…

That you will always believe in yourselves,
That you will always BE yourselves,
*And that you will always, **always** be free.*

Mom.

Be yourself;
everyone else is already taken.
—Oscar Wilde

PREFACE

I am pleased to introduce *Project Personal Freedom: Tips and Tools for a Liberated Life*, a year's worth of insights and action steps for finding the freedom so many of us seek—organized as daily entries for all 365 days of the year.

Over the years and across populations I've served—from addicts, codependents, and families in crisis, to the incarcerated, victims of natural disasters, and patients with terminal illnesses—certain challenges have consistently revealed themselves, as have the principles and practices clients have found to be most beneficial. My aim is to capture both the challenges and the "remedies," all under the umbrella of what I see as the overriding objective of my clients' journeys: personal freedom.

You don't have to fall into one of these groups to benefit from the daily entries in this book. You need not be struggling or in crisis of any kind. This book is about freedom. It is for everyone.

Personal freedom, as I see it, is an overall liberated life experience. It's a state of being in which one is self-determined and self-directed. It's the ability to explore, to dream, to self-define, and to be who one authentically is and be unapologetic about it. It's a state of mind. It's a way of life.

The tips and tools herein are by no means one person's perspective. They are inspired by those with whom I have worked over the years. They have revealed themselves as the concepts with which clients have most connected. They've also been at the heart of my own healing journey. I have simply pinpointed nuggets, packaged them up thematically, added insights from various schools of thought in psychology, and turned them into tips and tools for a liberated life.

Project Personal Freedom is born of the same motivation that inspired my grandfather George H. Gallup to create the American Institute of Public Opinion (which would become The Gallup Poll) over seventy-five years ago. Teddy, as he was affectionately known to us, was a true pioneer. Fiercely curious, with a heart for social service, he dedicated himself to creating avenues for hearing from the American people. This passion found its way into all he did.

All of this began with a simple philosophy, a heartfelt passion, and a deep hunger to know. I believe effective counselors are similarly motivated. We meet people where they are. We listen to their stories and hear their needs. We walk alongside them from that place.

Throughout his career, Teddy remained steadfastly committed to learning and reporting "the will of the people." This is my intention as well: to give back to my readers what I have learned is important to them, and in so doing, to meet them precisely where they are.

Project Personal Freedom is more than just a series of feel-good concepts. These are concrete, time-tested action steps. It's my hope that these daily pieces will be a source of comfort and inspiration and that this little book will be a helpful companion on your own journey to personal freedom.

INTRODUCTION
HOMEWARD BOUND

We shall not cease from exploration
And the end of all our exploring
Will be to arrive where we started
And know the place for the first time.
—T. S. Eliot

Welcome to your journey. It's a journey of rebirth, renewal, and restoration. It's an exploration of self. It's a celebration of personhood.

Personal freedom is pure authenticity. It's being freely and unapologetically you. It's who you've always been. It's also who you want to be again. Personal freedom is your birthright. Applying these daily tips will help you claim it.

This freedom is yours for the taking. You simply have to do the footwork. And the time is now.

Lean into who you are. Break free from anything that constricts and constrains. Choose to use your life-force wisely, channeling your energy into becoming your truest self. Do what makes you come alive. Design a life you love.

By dedicating yourself to this journey one reading at a time, a new and liberated life will take shape. As you align with your true nature, you will awaken to possibility and potential. You will feel alive and activated. You will discover happiness and fulfillment. Life will feel more like your own.

A rich and fulfilling existence awaits you as you embrace this process of becoming. You've wandered long enough. It's time to come home.

Welcome to your new beginning.

> *Twenty years from now you will be more disappointed by the things you didn't do than by the ones you did do. So throw off the bowlines. Sail away from the safe harbor. Catch the trade winds in your sails. Explore. Dream. Discover.*
> —Mark Twain

DAY 1
CLAIM YOUR FREEDOM

You were built for freedom. It's your primary nature. It's how you were meant to be.

The essence of freedom is free will. It is the ability to choose for ourselves and to take action independently of outside forces. It is autonomy, independence, and self-regulation. It's the right to be fully who we are.

You were born free. You were born with the potential to decide for yourself. Even in the most desperate situations, you always have choice. And where there is choice, there is freedom.

Repossess what's rightfully yours. Freedom is within you.

Man is free at the moment he wishes to be.
—Voltaire

DAY 2
DESIGN A LIFE YOU LOVE

Want a life you can feel good about? Then make your life a journey toward authenticity—a continual pursuit of personal truth.

You are the expert on *you*. If you don't think you are, become one. Only then can you follow your bliss. Only then can you know where your happiness is found. Only then can you be discerning about each and every choice you make along the way.

Designing a life you love will be a continuous creative endeavor. It will be your personal work in progress, your ongoing work of art.

Pursue an increasingly genuine existence. Start gathering data. Seek to understand yourself better. Stay curious, conscious, and teachable. Shape your own destiny.

You are the artist, and your life is your masterpiece. Design it exactly as you wish.

I have found that if you love life, life will love you back.
—Arthur Rubinstein

DAY 3
BE THE CHANGE

Be the change you want to experience in life. Don't wait. Don't wonder. Be it.

We tend to wait around for people and circumstances to change. We tell ourselves we will get what we want when they do. We think we will then be okay. When they don't change, we find ourselves bitter, disappointed, and resentful.

If you want change, be the change.

If you want respect, be respectful. If you want truth, be truthful. If you want intimacy, be intimate. If you want to feel connected, foster connections. If you want healing, be a healing presence. If you want joy, be joyful.

Stop waiting around and take action. Be whatever it is you want to experience.

To laugh often and much; to win the respect of intelligent people and the affection of children; to earn the appreciation of honest critics and endure the betrayal of false friends; to appreciate beauty, to find the best in others; to leave the world a bit better, whether by a healthy child, a garden patch or a redeemed social condition; to know even one life has breathed easier because you have lived. This is to have succeeded.
—Ralph Waldo Emerson

DAY 4
SHOW THE WORLD HOW WONDERFUL YOU ARE

Many of us hide our light, play small, and deny the wonder of who we are. We hold back all that's magnificent within us. Somehow we justify it in our own minds.

Perhaps we fear being too big for our britches. We don't want to seem self-aggrandizing or showy. We don't want others to feel uncomfortable around us. So we play ourselves down. We temper our talents and moderate our own glory.

You're doing yourself a profound injustice by diminishing who you are. You're also robbing the world of the wonder of *you*. Others deserve to experience the fullness of your character, not some watered-down version.

Break out of fear. Liberate yourself from the limitations that have confined and constricted you. Let go of all the modesty and be fabulous!

Freedom lies in being bold.
—Robert Frost

DAY 5
OUTGROW YOUR HISTORY

The best predictor of future behavior is past behavior. It's a pretty common notion. Popularized as it has been, it's not always a helpful philosophy. It leaves no room for growth and change. It makes no allowance for insight, awareness, and turnarounds.

If you've been living by this concept, you know it doesn't work. By forecasting the future based on the past, you lock yourself in, becoming your own self-fulfilling prophecy. The future becomes more of the same. For those of us who have struggled along the way, it's a setup for disappointment.

The best predictor of your future is not your past. Rather, it's how you learn and grow from your past. It's how you use your history.

Whatever your life has been, there is always hope for a new beginning. Break out of your history, shake off the past, and allow yourself a fresh start. Start living by a philosophy that helps you do so.

Your past is not your potential. Your past is your past. Pure and simple.

The farther behind I leave the past,
the closer I am to forging my own character.
—Isabelle Eberhardt

DAY 6
CHOOSE YOURSELF

Every choice along life's pathway is a crossroads—a chance to move closer to self or farther away, to stay on course or to head down a rabbit trail.

Whether big or small, significant or seemingly insignificant, each decision along the way matters. Each is an opportunity to honor who we are, to do what's authentic, to strengthen our connection with our core, and to learn even more about ourselves than we knew before.

Your own unique path is shaped one choice at a time. So too are your optimal outcomes.

When you find yourself at one of life's crossroads, ask yourself, "Does this bring me closer to who I am or farther away? Is it on my path or simply a diversion?"

With every move you make, do your best to stay on course. If you stray, get back on track.

Remember, your choices shape you. Respect the significance of each and every one of them.

Life is the sum of all your choices.
—Albert Camus

DAY 7
ASK WHAT MAKES YOU COME ALIVE

Many of us do things backwards. We look for fulfillment from the outside in. We seek direction from external sources. We let the world tell us who we need to be. It's a shaky way to live.

What if you took back your identity? What if you looked for satisfaction from the inside out instead? What if you sought direction from within? You're apt to find a stability of self like never before. You're likely to feel alive, empowered, and in charge of your own life.

The best path to contentment is to step into the truth of who you are, to lean into your authenticity, and to live from that place. It's also the only way to have a truly meaningful presence in this world.

The world needs you. You need *you*.

Do what you love. Know your own bone;
gnaw at it, bury it, unearth it, and gnaw it still.
—Henry David Thoreau

DAY 8
CREATE A LIFE THAT FITS YOU BETTER

Things don't seem to be flowing. You're feeling dissatisfied. You know something is wrong, but you're not sure what. It could be your life just isn't a fit.

Maybe you've always been that square peg in a round hole, shapeshifting to live by a set of standards that are not your own. Perhaps you've been denying who you are, disowning aspects of yourself. Maybe your life has never felt like your own. You might be asking what I asked myself for years: "Who's living my life anyway?"

It's time to create a life that fits you better. It's time to take responsibility for your present and your future. No more sublimating self. No more going through the motions, maintaining the status quo, and letting habit determine how you do things.

Trust yourself. If it feels like your life doesn't fit, odds are it doesn't. Start picturing what would be a match.

The time is now. Step into a life you love.

You are not the momentary whim of a careless creator experimenting
in the laboratory of life. . . You were made with a purpose.
—Og Mandino

DAY 9
CELEBRATE UNIQUENESS

One size doesn't fit all. Thinking it does only frustrates and restricts.

You are an individual. You are special. You have distinct wants and needs, thoughts and feelings, passions and dreams. If you've been boxing yourself in, trying to fit into some standard set of norms, it's time to make a change.

Stop telling yourself you have to live your life as others live theirs. Don't fight your uniqueness. Lean into it instead.

Align with your true nature. Live life as you were meant to live it. One size won't do!

At bottom every man knows well enough that he is a unique being,
only once on this earth; and by no extraordinary chance will
such a marvelously picturesque piece of diversity in unity
as he is, ever be put together a second time.
—Friedrich Nietzsche

DAY 10
RECLAIM YOUR IDENTITY

Have you lost ownership of yourself? If so, it's time to reclaim it.

To reclaim is to retrieve, restore, or repossess. To reclaim is to take back sovereignty over something or someone. This journey of personal freedom is one of taking back possession of our own identities. It's our personal reclamation project.

For me, this concept has been nothing short of life-changing. Little did I know my job wasn't to change myself, but rather to *be* myself!

Embrace this journey of liberation. Free yourself from the bondage of history, limitation, outside expectations, and anything that has co-opted your sense of self. Own again what you have disowned. Put yourself back on your rightful course.

It's time to reclaim your identity. It was meant to be yours anyway.

It is never too late to be who you might have been.
—George Elliot

DAY 11
GET SERIOUS ABOUT LOVING YOURSELF

Loving yourself is more than a warm fuzzy. Loving yourself is serious business.

Many of us look at self-love as indulgent and self-serving. We see it as a frivolous luxury, some fluffy undertaking meant to make us feel comfy inside. In reality, it's a very practical matter.

Learning to love ourselves is about taking responsibility for our relationship with ourselves. It's breaking out of a victim mindset and getting proactive on our own behalf. It's bringing a higher, healthier version of you to the table in life.

Step up to the plate and honor yourself. Don't wait around for others to do it. Claim your birthright of self-love. There's nothing silly or indulgent about it.

It is of practical value to learn to like yourself.
Since you must spend so much time with yourself you
might as well get some satisfaction out of the relationship.
—Norman Vincent Peale

DAY 12
BUILD YOUR FOUNDATION

Being raised with instability affects us. Growing up with unpredictability, inconsistency, and chaos inhibits the development of a solid core and a sense of grounding and sure-footedness. Our foundation is weak. It was laid on shaky ground.

Early on in life we needed our environment to be our stability. We needed this so we could explore and evolve, stretch and grow, and do so steadily and consistently. Without this, we felt unsteady inside. This shakiness eventually showed itself in our lives. We began playing out the effects of an unstable foundation.

Perhaps you have never experienced true stability. Maybe you have been ungrounded in some of the most critical areas, such as self-worth, integrity, personal autonomy, boundaries, and a fundamental belief in yourself.

Now that you're awakened to this, you can change. You get to begin giving yourself what you didn't get then. You can build your foundation anew.

Build it on solid ground this time.

To put it bluntly, I seem to have a whole superstructure
with no foundation. But I'm working on the foundation.
—Marilyn Monroe

DAY 13
BE WHAT YOU SEEM

Be authentic. It's a pretty basic concept, but one by which many of us don't live.

Instead of being who we are, we play to the audience. We show one face to the world and we turn our true face inward. We resist authenticity. We live painfully incongruent lives.

Rather than trying to figure out which face to wear—and when to wear it—just be yourself. Pursue harmony between your inner and outer worlds. Be what you seem.

It sure makes things simpler.

Who we are looking for is who is looking.
—Francis of Assisi

DAY 14
BE A KID WITH NO BAGGAGE

Kids are enviably unburdened. My son and daughter have an innocent and infectious lightness about them—a natural buoyancy. They live purely in the moment, unfettered by yesterday. Wouldn't it be wonderful, as adults, to recapture that feeling? To let go of all the baggage we have been lugging around?

Emotional baggage might be the remnants of a past trauma, a painful childhood environment, or a previous relationship. Whatever the origin, it influences our experience of life and becomes a distorted lens through which we interpret our world.

In clinging to past hurts and negative messages about ourselves, we live in reaction to life. We recreate situations that don't serve us. We become cynical, discouraged, and drained.

Identify your baggage. Explore its roots. Make a decision to individuate from your history and from what happened to you. Tap back into the way you came into this world—precious, worthy, and valuable.

You are powerless to rewrite your past. But you can frame it differently. You can live a life of your choosing, as opposed to a life your history chose for you.

Let go of the past and step into the present. Become that unencumbered kid again.

Whatever your past has been, you have a spotless future.
—Author unknown

DAY 15
SHAPE YOUR FUTURE ONE *TODAY* AT A TIME

We can get incredibly overwhelmed by the prospect of change. We look ahead and feel intimidated by the enormity of what we think needs to happen. In doing so, we miss what's right in front of us. We fail to see the power of today.

Healthy outcomes don't require big, sweeping pronouncements or dramatic promises of change. They aren't achieved with all-or-nothing thinking.

If you want to live your best possible life, rein yourself in, put your energy in the now, and remember that futures are built one *today* at a time.

There's no need to feel buried by the weight of needed change. For today, be your healthiest and highest possible self. The future will take it from there.

Real generosity toward the future lies in giving all to the present.
—Albert Camus

DAY 16
LIVE LIFE ON PURPOSE

Do you feel as if you're spinning your wheels? Expending all sorts of energy getting nowhere? Have you ever really thought about the pupose of your life? It might be time for a mission.

A personal mission statement is a powerful exercise in harnessing passion and potential and channeling these into a life you love. A mission statement illuminates your personal truth. It tells you how to spend your human currency. It enables you to be deliberate about the life you live, rather than living a life you've been handed.

What do I want from my life? What do I value? Where are my talents? As I reflect on life's journey, what do I wish to have accomplished?

Set your sights on a direction in this life. Give your journey legs to stand on. Offer yourself measures of achievement so you can know you're walking in line with your passions, living your highest purpose, and contributing your very best to your world.

No more traveling through life without a roadmap. Create your mission, and let it guide you. The things you think about the most become your reality.

Don't ask what the world needs. Ask what makes you come alive. And go do it. Because what the world needs are people who have come alive.
—Howard Thurman

DAY 17
MAKE SOMETHING OF EVERY DAY

Every day has its purpose. Make the most of it.

Whether it's learning something new, stretching yourself a little, making a human connection, extending a kindness to someone, expressing a truth, or simply laughing a good laugh, each day is significant. Don't squander it.

It's so easy to get complacent. It's so easy to let the days slip by, simply going through the motions. Over time it becomes a source of great regret. Life isn't lived by hindsight, and you can't get back the days you've misspent. Embrace them as they come.

Get hungry for the promise of each day. Your life will be richer for it.

This is the beginning of a new day. You have been given this day to use as you will. You can waste it or use it for good. What you do today is important because you are exchanging a day of your life for it. When tomorrow comes, this day will be gone forever; in its place is something that you have left behind…let it be something good.
—Author unknown

DAY 18
LOOK WITHIN

Are you a grass-is-greener person? Do you tell yourself things are better on the other side?

As you look over that proverbial fence into your neighbor's yard, envying what's on the other side, you check out of your own life. You focus your attention out there somewhere, rather than within. You step out of gratitude. You step out of power. You enter the land of "I'd be happy if only...."

But nothing gets accomplished by yearning for someone else's life. If you want to get things done, be fulfilled, and flourish in this life, do the counterintuitive thing: want your own life, only better.

Stop looking over the fence. Plug into your own life, and tap into your own power. Make your own grass green.

Each one of us must live the life God gives him; it cannot be shirked.
                              —Sophocles

DAY 19
USE THOSE DISAPPOINTMENTS

Ah, disappointment. It's darn uncomfortable. It's raw, it's vulnerable, and it's humbling. It's something we all face. It's a universal condition. The difference among us lies in how we deal with it.

We can't change past circumstances; they've already happened. What we can do is choose how to respond to these circumstances. This is where our power is. This is where we find the distinction between disappointment that fuels us and disappointment that sets us back.

Don't let disappointment stop you in your tracks. Don't let it disempower you. Use disappointment. Burn it as fuel for your journey.

Life is like photography; we develop from the negatives.
—Author unknown

DAY 20
START ANEW

Someone once said to me, "You can start a new twenty-four hours anytime." I never forgot it.

How often we boldly pronounce, "Tomorrow I will quit." "Tomorrow I will start my new plan." Tomorrow comes, and by noon we have already broken our promise. Seeing the day as ruined, we abandon the remainder of the day. We can always try again tomorrow.

What if, instead of throwing in the towel and waiting for tomorrow's clean slate, you gave yourself a new twenty-four hours right away? What if you relinquished that extreme thinking, forgave yourself for being imperfect, and got right back on track?

Living in a mindset of all or nothing, good or bad, or black or white is no way to live. To be in your own good graces one minute and out of them the next is inconsistent and unfair.

There is a softer way. Dust yourself off and start again. You can do it anytime.

Failure is only the opportunity to begin again, only this time more wisely.
—Henry Ford

DAY 21
LET GO OF OUTCOMES

Trying to control outcomes only distorts who we are. As we seek to bring about favorable reactions in others—as we try to avoid the unfavorable—we end up living in bondage to end results.

Liberate yourself from this dependence. Ask for what you want and need. Let go of the outcome. Speak your truth. Let go of the outcome. Let others know who you are. Let go of the outcome.

This doesn't mean we barrel our way through life selfishly and thoughtlessly, blissfully unaware of how others feel. It simply means we know where—and over whom—we do and do not have power. We know the best we can offer any situation is our most authentic self. We place personal integrity over people-pleasing, knowing our number one job is to be genuine.

Give it a try. Let go of that attachment to outcomes. It's an infinitely more liberated way to live.

The most exhausting thing in life is being insincere.
—Anne Morrow Lindbergh

DAY 22
LEARN WHAT YOU'RE RUNNING FROM

On the road to personal freedom, we seek and we escape. We move toward and we move away.

Freedom is more than breaking away from something oppressive. Freedom is deliberate movement toward something liberating. It's knowing what we want and it's being unapologetic about going after it. It's proactive, not simply reactive.

To achieve freedom, you must first identify the forces from which you're pushing back. You have to face your fears in order to heal your demons. You have to know what you don't want in order to figure out what you do want. Then you can get proactive. Then you can begin designing a life that fits you better.

Knowing what you want, you can go after it.

All men should strive
to learn before they die
what they are running from, and to, and why.
—James Thurber

DAY 23
BE THE SAME INSIDE AND OUT

If you seem like someone you're not, or if you're not who you seem to be, something has to change.

Keeping up appearances takes a lot of energy. Choosing who to be and which face to wear is a lot to pull off. Life ends up feeling like a continuous performance. The inauthenticity is exhausting.

Living congruently, on the other hand, is enlivening. Being the same person inside and out doesn't require nearly the energy or fore-thought that living incongruently requires.

Make what you think and feel the same as what you say and do. Be true to yourself and honest with others. Be the person you are.

> *This above all:*
> *To thine own self be true,*
> *And it must follow, as the night the day,*
> *Thou canst not then be false to any man.*
> —Shakespeare

DAY 24
BEGIN

"Just begin." It was some of the best advice I ever received.

Stop with all the deadlines. Think about giving yourself start lines instead. Focus on beginning, rather than boxing yourself in with limits and cutoff dates. For anyone struggling with procrastination, this mental shift can be helpful.

We tend to focus so much on what we have to do— and when it has to be done—that we overwhelm ourselves into inaction. We create such mountains before us, we never actually begin whatever it is we want or need to do. We feel badly about ourselves for our inactivity.

What if, instead of freaking ourselves out with deadlines, we simply began? What if, instead of waiting and wondering, we took action— any action? If you're a writer, write. If you're a painter, paint. If there is something you need to do, just begin.

Push through that resistance and procrastination and stop delaying, especially when it's your dreams you're putting on hold.

Just begin.

We cannot do everything at once, but we can do something at once.
—Calvin Coolidge

DAY 25
LISTEN TO THE DIVINE DISCOMFORT

It's natural to want to escape discomfort. But not all uneasiness deserves to be avoided.

There is a divine kind of discomfort that calls us to attention. It's that strong desire within us to evolve, to stretch ourselves, to find greater expression of our authenticity, to explore, to create, and to blossom. It's a stirring in our hearts. It's there to motivate and inspire us.

Pay attention to that restlessness within. Attend to the divine discomfort, however uncomfortable or demanding it may seem. Make friends with it.

Your true self is calling. Make sure you listen.

And the day came when the risk to remain tight in a bud
was more painful than the risk it took to blossom.
—Anais Nin

DAY 26
WATCH THE FUTURE–TRIPPING

Sometimes we focus on the future to our detriment. We dwell in it. We get frenzied because of it. We check out of the now in our fixation on it. It's basically a matter of fear.

Fear not only steals from today, it lies to us about tomorrow. We become preoccupied with fear-based what ifs. We predict a negative tomorrow. We look at our future through doubting eyes.

None of us knows what tomorrow will bring. So let go of that fear. Let go of the illusion that all your future-tripping is somehow productive. Free up the energy you've been expending on those negative predictions. Spend it on today instead.

You won't bring about positive outcomes through rumination and anticipation. You bring them about by plugging into today.

Show up and engage in your life. Don't give in to that fear.

Don't take tomorrow to bed with you.
—Norman Vincent Peale

DAY 27
SWEEP YOUR PORCH

It's essential we own our own stuff, take responsibility for ourselves, and make the changes in our own behavior that need to be made. It's our duty to do this for ourselves. It isn't our duty to do it for anyone else.

Your job is *you*. There is something empowering and liberating about taking care of your own business and letting go of how others are or are not taking care of theirs.

You are your own change agent. So focus on what you can do rather than what you can't. Put your focus where your power is. Let go of the illusion that you have to sweep anyone's porch but your own.

If you have been doing more than your share, liberate yourself with this one realization:

It's okay to stop.

Freedom is the will to be responsible to ourselves.
—Friedrich Nietzsche

DAY 28
PUT DOWN THE BAGS

We lug around all sorts of emotional baggage. It weighs us down. It drains our life force. So why do it? Why carry feelings that don't belong to us?

Somewhere along the way we must have learned it was our job to be emotional receptacles. We got the impression we were responsible for other people's wellbeing. We learned to caretake. We believed it was our duty to do so. Anything less would be selfish and unloving.

But these are the beliefs of codependence. These are the beliefs of a person who learned to source worth and value through others, to find significance through caretaking, and to self-deny and self-abandon rather than care for self. These patterns are neither loving nor noble.

It's time to put down the baggage you've been carrying. It's time to release the emotional burden. There is nothing healthy about lugging around what isn't yours; it only clouds your own emotional self.

It's okay to lighten the load.

Cherish your own emotions and never undervalue them.
—Robert Henri

DAY 29
LOVE YOURSELF

We seem to think it's possible for people to love us in place of our loving ourselves. It's actually impossible. Sure, we all want people to love us for who we are, but trying to adopt other people's feelings for us as our own is tricky business.

We crave external love because we don't love ourselves. We become dependent on other-esteem because we don't have self-esteem. We look for our worth and our value outside ourselves because we aren't sourcing it from within. We seek validation, as it distracts us from the painful reality that we don't validate ourselves.

No one can love you in place of *you*. No one can complete you if you don't feel complete within. No one can keep you comfortable enough *not* to feel the state of your own self-esteem.

Stop looking for love in all the wrong places. Stop buying into the illusion that others can love you for you. It's your job and yours alone.

To love oneself is the beginning of a life-long romance.
—Oscar Wilde

DAY 30
PRACTICE DISCERNMENT

If you want to live a life you love, you will have to be shrewd about it.

Be selective about what you take into your life and what you don't, about the people you engage with and those you don't, about where you apply your energy and where you don't, and about every choice you make.

We might not have had a say early on in life about our environment, about what influenced us, and about the forces that acted upon us each and every day, but today we do have a say. And today we have a responsibility to create for ourselves an environment that supports a healthy, satisfying existence.

To live a truly liberated life you will need to be discriminating about every aspect of it. Be choosy. Be shrewd.

If you aren't discerning about your life, who will be?

It's not hard to make decisions when you know what your values are.
—Roy Disney

DAY 31
KEEP THE FAITH

The good balances with the bad…and the bad with the good. It might not always be in equal proportion—at least not in the short term—but things do have a way of balancing out.

One of the best remedies for managing pain and hardship is to begin looking for the good that's right around the corner. Perhaps it's right in front of you already. Maybe it's yet to come.

I like to track blessings that show themselves in my life, usually jotting them in my day timer. I find myself struck by their divine timing and how often they come right on the heels of something painful. The good really does balance with the bad.

In many ways, this is a gratitude practice. It's about choosing what you magnify. It's about paying attention. There is joy all around if your eyes are open to see it.

Embrace both the good and the bad, knowing they have an interesting way of working together. It's all part of the human experience.

Had a run of bad luck? A period of adversity? Start looking for the good. You're sure to find it.

When one door of happiness closes, another opens,
but often we look so long at the closed door that we
do not see the one that has been opened up for us.
—Helen Keller

DAY 32
KNOW YOU'RE WORTHY

If you have been burning yourself out trying to be worthy, you're likely feeling a sense of futility about it all.

When we don't feel worthy at our core, we try to make up for our perceived unworthiness. We drive ourselves to achieve. We perform and we please. We do our very best to be good. While there are some temporary payoffs along the way, in the long run our efforts fall short.

The truth is, you are worthy. You always have been. Any attempts to earn worth and value have been in vain because these simply can't be earned—they were never meant to be.

There is nothing to make up for—because what you're trying to make up for you've had all along.

I wish I could show you when you are lonely or in darkness
the astonishing light of your own being.
—Hafiz of Persia

DAY 33
GO TO THE PLACES THAT SCARE YOU

We all try to avoid things that scare us; it's natural to do so. But avoidance can become a way of life. Evasion can permeate our life experience, blocking us from living and learning.

We all have struggles. The danger is letting life become *the* struggle. We can become so consumed by resistance that we make ourselves unavailable to all that's good in our lives. We can also miss the powerful lessons in the not-so-good.

Stop resisting. Lean into your experience and learn from it. Triumph over that fear.

He who is not every day conquering some
fear has not learned the secret of life.
—Ralph Waldo Emerson

DAY 34
LOOK FOR THE SWEET SPOT

Do you live life in extremes? Do you see things as black or white, good or bad, right or wrong, or all or nothing?

It's an unstable and exhausting way to live. In the up moments, life is intense and exciting. In the down moments, it's lifeless and depressing. The pendulum swings broadly from one extreme to another. This polarization creates distress and instability within.

Living life in black and white can be symptomatic of a self-esteem issue. When we don't feel worthy and valuable at our core—when our sense of self is fragile and fleeting—we end up living unbalanced lives. We live life on the outside, always trying to feed ourselves because we feel hollow within. We hunt for fulfillment. We push and push and inevitably shut down. There is no consistency of self.

Life isn't meant to be lived in extremes. It isn't meant to be all or nothing—wonderful at times and disastrous at others. Peace is found in the middle ground. It is in balance where we experience serenity and security, where we feel empowered, and where we don't have to prove anything to anyone—including ourselves.

No more living that unbalanced life. Live in that sweet spot instead. It's somewhere in the middle.

Keep a mid course between two extremes.
—Ovid

DAY 35
FEED YOURSELF

Have you been starving yourself? Have you been withholding the very things you know satisfy you? Have you been ignoring your desires, telling yourself you should be satisfied with less?

Stop thinking it's somehow noble to go hungry. There's nothing wrong with having a big appetite for life. There's nothing wrong with feeding yourself, giving yourself attention, and doing what you love.

Go ahead: satisfy yourself. Take a big fat bite out of your life.

If we all did the things we are capable of doing,
we would literally astound ourselves.
—Thomas Edison

DAY 36
DECONSTRUCT THE CONSTRUCTED PERSONALITY

Many of us construct a personality to help us get by in this world. Subconsciously over time, we collect a host of protective mechanisms and assemble a persona. It's a self we believe will be lovable and accepted—one that will buffer us from discomfort and help us survive. For a while, this constructed personality seems to work.

Over time, however, it turns against us. We come to realize we are leading a double life. We sense incongruence between our inner and outer worlds. We are one person inside and another on the outside. The personality we constructed in order to survive is now keeping us from thriving. It is boxing us in and preventing us from connecting with life in a meaningful, authentic way.

If you want to live a liberated life, deconstruct that constructed personality. Identify your coping mechanisms, acknowledge their futility, get committed to living more authentically, and learn how to truly thrive.

Let go of the façade, and get real.

The privilege of a lifetime is to become who you truly are.
—Carl Jung

DAY 37
CLEAR THE BLOCKS

Do you feel blocked? Stunted? Do you wonder why life seems difficult—why it doesn't seem to flow?

There are likely some pockets of resistance within you, based on messages you've been telling yourself for some time now. Perhaps you're carrying around perceived limitations about what you can and can't do. Feelings of discouragement and pessimism could be dragging you down.

For a long time, I believed the resistance. If it was there and if it was speaking to me, I assumed it must be legitimate.

These are the painful remnants of past wounding, and they contribute to that lack of flow you're feeling. They impede momentum. They slow you down and hold you back.

Freedom hinges on your ability to identify and clear these blocks. Only then can you liberate true self. Only then can you live the life that you have only dreamed—the life you were meant to live.

Clear the blocks, and let life flow.

Tension is who you think you should be; relaxation is who you are.
—Chinese proverb

DAY 38
CARVE OUT PEACE FOR YOURSELF

Each of us gets to create our serenity in this world.

No matter what our current status is, we can have a sense of peace. We can have it anywhere, in any circumstance, and with anyone, for it comes from within.

Creating and holding on to inner tranquility requires healthy personal boundaries. It hinges on our ability to protect and safeguard ourselves. It's being discerning about what we take into our inner reality and what we don't.

Be intentional. Carve out your inner peace. Guard that serenity.

It's within your power to do.

Peace comes from within. Do not seek it without.
—Buddha

DAY 39
BE WHO YOU ARE, NOT WHO YOU THINK YOU SHOULD BE

Do you feel like you've been fighting and pushing your way through life? Like life is an uphill battle? Like you've been swimming upstream?

Chances are, instead of being who you are, you have been trying to fit into some mold of who you think you should be. You've been trying to fit your life into a prescribed set of rules. You clearly don't fit into them, but you keep trying.

Being who you think you should be is exhausting. It's also a setup for feeling perpetually disappointed. How could feel anything but? You're not meant to be anyone other than who you are. Trying to be someone else means you will always fall short of the mark.

Be *you* instead. You're bound to feel like a success.

Let the world know you as you are, not as you think you should be,
because sooner or later, if you are posing, you will forget the pose,
and then where are you?
—Fanny Brice

DAY 40
ABSTAIN FROM CHAOS

Are you a crisis junkie? Is chaos your drug of choice?

Many of us depend on chaos—thrive on it even. When it isn't readily available, we drum it up. We think we need it in order to feel engaged and alive.

But chaos isn't all it's cracked up to be. Chaos won't give you meaning or purpose. Chaos isn't living. Chaos is simply chaos. It distracts you from *you*, and it drains your life force. If you're hooked on it, it's time to get unhooked.

Detach from chaos. Notice its presence in your life and how it doesn't serve you. When you see yourself getting caught up in it again, step back, take a breath, and think about where it leads.

Soon you will appreciate a newfound freedom. You will feel more secure, serene, and balanced. You will respond to life, rather than react to it. You will become increasingly unwilling to invite chaos into your life again.

Resist that chaos compulsion. You will be glad you did.

*It is often tragic to see how blatantly a man bungles his own life
and the lives of others, yet remains totally incapable of seeing
how much the whole tragedy originates in himself, and how
he continually feeds it and keeps it going.*
—Carl Jung

DAY 41
ACCEPT THE ACCEPTABLE

Think about the messages you send yourself when you tolerate the intolerable, accept the unacceptable, and withstand what you know isn't okay. Think about what you've been putting up with and why.

Look closely and you'll see why you do this. You'll see that what you've been allowing—even inviting—into your life is a match with what you think and feel about yourself. You accept the unacceptable because somehow it fits. You must not believe you deserve better.

If you devalue yourself, others will devalue you. If you disrespect yourself, you will be disrespected. If you treat yourself poorly, other people will follow suit.

This has been an enormous wake up call in my own healing journey. More disturbing than all the dynamics in which I felt mistreated was the fact that I was pretty oblivious to it all—or at least unwilling to do anything about it. Due to my own perceived unworthiness, I had been silently sanctioning the treatment I was receiving.

Since you attract what you believe you deserve, it's time to start telling yourself you deserve better. Mistreatment needs to be a mismatch, not a perfect fit.

Clean up your relationship with *you* and start attracting what you truly deserve.

They cannot take away our self-respect if we do not give it to them.
—Mahatma Gandhi

DAY 42
WATCH THE LINEAR PERSPECTIVE

Many of us white-knuckle it through life. We hold our breath, hoping and praying we will continue on our chosen course. We seem to think we need to follow some unbroken path to enlightenment and achievement. We live in fear of getting derailed. We live in fear of a slip.

In time, our humanness shows. We have a weak moment. We make a mistake. And back to square one we go—or so we think.

It seems we have adopted a common point of view—one that says we can move seamlessly from one stage of life to the next. When we stumble, we think, "Now I have to start all over," and "I had come so far; I can't believe I'm here again!" This perspective creates undue pressure. It's a setup for being disappointed in ourselves.

We are dynamic creatures, ever changing and ever learning, and life is a process. It's a journey, not a destination. And the journey is anything but linear. Each bump in the road is a challenge. It's a chance to propel ourselves into an even better place. It's not a setback. It's an opportunity to grow.

Let go of that linear perspective. Let go of the need for perfection. If you're going to ask anything of yourself, ask that you learn with each experience, that you make the most of it all, and that with each challenge, you come closer to who you are.

Success consists of getting up just one more time than you fall.
—Oliver Goldsmith

DAY 43
TAKE A CHANCE

If you have been craving something new, yearning for a different kind of life, or continually commenting on the dissatisfaction you feel, ask yourself, "What have I done about it? Have I taken action to change things?" Or has wanting something different become a chronic condition?

It doesn't have to be. If you want a new experience, create one. If you want change, make it happen. If you want a new life, go out and get it.

Don't let the old thinking rob you of the new life you seek. Push through fear. Break out of resistance. Get unstuck.

What are you waiting for?

I dip my pen in the blackest ink,
because I'm not afraid of falling into my inkpot.
—Ralph Waldo Emerson

DAY 44
ENJOY YOUR OWN COMPANY

Many of us run from being alone.

Perhaps we have been deriving our sense of worth, value, and direction externally, from the outside-in, and we don't know what to do with ourselves in our aloneness. We feel empty, bewildered, and purposeless.

But being alone doesn't have to be uncomfortable. Our discomfort has more to do with what we think about ourselves and how we interpret our aloneness.

The healthier your relationship with yourself, the more you will embrace the "you" time. You will stop judging it and begin using it wisely. You will find yourself looking forward to it.

Learn to enjoy the company you keep in those alone moments.

I love to be alone. I never found the companion
that was so companionable as solitude.
—Henry David Thoreau

DAY 45
SAY THANK YOU

Perspective is paramount. How we interpret our lives, especially the seemingly negative elements of life, means absolutely everything. To say thank you for it all is to be enlightened.

Every experience is an opportunity to wake up and grow up. Every challenge is a chance to become transformed. The more we say *thank you*, the more we evolve.

That being said, each of us experiences certain things for which it seems impossible to say thank you. In such cases, we don't have to thank the circumstance directly. Maybe it's the potential for growth for which we can be thankful. Maybe it's the possibilities the experience generates for which we can give thanks.

Life changes when we adopt this mindset—this vision. We stay open to life experience, ever curious about what we can learn and how we can grow.

You have the power to shift your perspective. You have the power to live in a spirit of that existential "thank you."

Some people are always grumbling because roses have thorns;
I am thankful that thorns have roses.
—Alphonse Karr

DAY 46
PUT PRINCIPLES FIRST

We can get so caught up in human dynamics that we miss out on what matters. We get distracted—even consumed—by the ins and outs of our interactions with others. We let them engulf us. We let them change who we are and who we want to be.

Putting personalities over principles is risky. By getting caught up in the superficial, we miss out on what's meaningful. We betray ourselves and our value systems. We get stuck in resentment and frustration because we never go deeper than the data. We react rather than respond to life.

Put principles over personalities instead and everything changes. Instead of giving your energy over to situations and circumstances, you protect and preserve it, using it as you choose. You are internally directed rather than externally driven. You are deliberate and proactive, letting your values dictate how you respond to life. You show up as you intend to show up, not as your current situation drives you to.

Make sure you have your priorities straight. Put principles over personalities. Be the person you intend to be.

There is a natural principle of benevolence in man, which is in some degree to society what self-love is to the individual.
—Joseph Butler

DAY 47
FOCUS FORWARD

Our lives would look very different if, instead of dragging along the past as a basis for constant comparison, we lived life today forward. No more looking back or measuring today against yesterday—just embracing and making the most of the *now*.

All too often we try to recapture history. We think about what was and wonder why we can't get back there. Our retrospection keeps us from showing up and plugging in.

Today is where your power is. Today is the time for change. When you see yourself glancing back, focus forward again. Redirect your attention, and keep your eyes straight ahead.

Treat life—and your circumstances as they exist today—as a gift you were just handed. Now what are you going to do with it?

If you focus on what's left behind,
you'll never be able to see what lies ahead.
—Author unknown

DAY 48
FACE THE FINAL FRONTIER

Ah, family of origin. It's our first environment. It's our most formative experience. It's our final frontier.

It's in our family of origin where we formed our basic beliefs about ourselves. It's where we learned about personal boundaries, communication, and relationships. It's where we were taught about growth and potential, where we developed emotionally, mentally, and spiritually. It's where our life perspective was shaped.

If some of your family ties feel unhealthy, address them. Turn toward your past, especially if it's part of your present. Get deliberate about breaking free from what's holding you back. If you choose to look your past in the eye, there is much to be learned. There is growth to be had. Ignoring it won't work.

Your family of origin formed you, and it remains a powerful classroom. Don't leave this part of your life unexamined. Every bit of it has value.

The family. We were a strange little band of characters trudging through life sharing diseases and toothpaste, coveting one another's desserts, hiding shampoo, borrowing money, locking each other out of our rooms, inflicting pain and kissing to heal it in the same instant, loving, laughing, defending, and trying to figure out the common thread that bound us all together.
—Erma Bombeck

DAY 49
LIGHTEN UP

Do you feel heavy, burdened, and uninspired? Is it hard to find the good in life? You could be taking yourself too seriously.

Perhaps you're bogging yourself down with too many *shoulds*, *ought tos*, and *have tos*. Maybe your outlook is distorted by pessimism and lingering disappointments. You might be in the habit of being hard on yourself.

You can find the good and the not-so-good in just about everything. So choose to focus on the good. Let go of the beliefs that bind you. Bring hope and enthusiasm to every circumstance of your life. When you do, the way you experience life will change.

Lighten up and look for the good.

Do not take life too seriously. You will never get out of it alive.
—Elbert Hubbard

DAY 50
KNOW YOURSELF

"You are the expert on you," I was once told. What a concept!

You know your heart. You know your passions and interests. You know your likes and dislikes. You know exactly who you are—you've always known. But it doesn't mean you have acted on it.

What we often do instead is make others the experts on who we are. We adopt their perspectives and accept their impressions of us as our own. We allow them to steer our own course. We let them tell us who to be and who not to be. We give them that power.

All the information you need is within you. Stop looking outside yourself to find yourself. Take back ownership over your own identity.

You are the expert on you. You have all the answers. You always have.

No one knows you like you do.

That's the way things come clear. All of a sudden.
And then you realize how obvious they've been all along.
—Madeleine L'Engle

DAY 51
GET FEISTY

If we turn toward our histories with motivation and resolve, promising ourselves to learn from the past and to do things differently moving forward, we come to see how our histories have shaped us. We learn how to break free.

Addressing dysfunction, past or present, challenges us to look at ourselves and how we have been living our lives. It calls us to action. In rescuing ourselves and recovering our autonomy, we build serious muscle. We develop aspects of ourselves that could have easily remained undeveloped. We build new life skills and become stronger than we ever imagined. We come to see we are better for it all.

Your history doesn't define you. It doesn't dictate who you will become, and it doesn't determine your life path. You need not be destined to repeat the themes of your past.

Get feisty. What challenges you most only makes you more determined.

The truth is that our finest moments are most likely to occur when we are feeling deeply uncomfortable, unhappy, or unfulfilled. For it is only in such moments, propelled by our discomfort, that we are likely to step out of our ruts and start searching for different ways or truer answers.
—Author unknown

DAY 52
FEEL

Feelings are energy. This emotional energy is always moving, changing, and flowing through us—if we let it, that is.

All too often, however, we fight our own feelings. We hold our breath, trapping that emotional energy inside of us. We push back from whatever it is we don't want to feel because we fear our own feelings. We give them power. We are afraid they will last forever.

Truth is, in fighting our emotions, we bring about the very emotional stuck-ness we fear. We become all the more attached to our feelings. Whatever we suppress, deny, or minimize will simply stick around all the more.

Emotions are like a river. When we let them flow, we feel clear and clean. When we dam them up, we feel dark and murky. This applies to life experiences as well. When in the midst of an uncomfortable experience, we think it will last forever—but it never does.

Be *with* the feelings and they will change. It's paradoxical but true. Own your emotions and the energy will shift.

Let yourself feel badly in order to feel good again.

Eyes that do not cry, do not see.
—Swedish proverb

DAY 53
DEFINE YOURSELF

Many of us have allowed our histories to define us. And because of it, we have yet to fully emerge from the past.

Whatever the case, your history has affected you. Perhaps it handed you some ill-fitting labels—and you adopted them. Maybe you have been wearing them ever since. They have a way of becoming self-ful-filling prophecies.

Here's the good news: You are not what your history said you were. Yes, your history affected you, perhaps in deeply painful ways. But, your history does not define you. You define you.

Commit yourself to breaking out of the mold. No one gets to define you but you.

To be nobody but yourself in a world which is doing its best, night and day, to make you everybody else means to fight the hardest battle which any human being can fight; and never stop fighting.
—E. E. Cummings

DAY 54
COME TO YOUR OWN ASSISTANCE

Each of us has the ability to help ourselves. Each of us has the potential to pull ourselves up and out of those holes we inevitably fall into at times.

We all have pain. We all slip into uncomfortable, wounded places. The question is, how do we show up for ourselves when this happens?

We need not stay in the darkness. We can heal ourselves. We have more of a say in the duration of our sorrowful states than we may realize.

You are an emotional being. You are vulnerable, and you will hurt sometimes. You can't be human and avoid this. The key is to make sure you have a loving inner parent—a functional adult within—who rises up when you need it. Make sure you meet yourself where you are and love yourself in that space. Not doing so only prolongs the pain.

Be good to yourself. Look after yourself. And whatever you do, come to your own assistance.

Pain is inevitable; suffering is optional.
—Author unknown

DAY 55
BECOME YOURSELF

In Eastern traditions, the lotus flower is a symbol of the human journey.

The lotus flower grows in the mud, eventually emerging in beautiful splendor. In the same way, we grow in the mud of life's challenges and hardships. We surface in our own magnificence.

Your journey is one of steady growth. Your experiences inform and instruct your evolution. They fertilize and form you. By remaining open and teachable, you become increasingly authentic, growing into the fullness of your beauty.

Allow your life to be a process of unfolding. Gain wisdom as you go. Your life is like a lotus flower.

I embrace emerging experience.
I participate in discovery.
I am a butterfly.
I am not a butterfly collector.
I want the experience of the butterfly.
—William Stafford

DAY 56
CATCH UP WITH YOU

Many of us try anything and everything to escape ourselves. We run. We hide. We busy ourselves. We avoid who we are. We may not even know we are doing it.

Trying to outrun yourself disconnects you from your core. Keeping your vulnerability—the part of you you're likely trying to outrun—a secret only stigmatizes you further in your own eyes. In trying to escape yourself, you contribute to your own internal woundedness.

You can't outrun yourself and expect to be happy. You can't successfully beat your pain, or any uncomfortable emotion, without at some point looking it square in the eye and dealing with it. The emotion will simply grow within you.

What if you made a decision to stop running? What if you slowed down and got current with yourself? Freedom requires that you turn your attention inward and get honest.

You can't outrun yourself forever. Your truth will catch up with you. Why not turn and embrace it?

Be what you are. This is the first step
towards becoming better than you are.
—J. C. Hare & A. W. Hare

DAY 57
GROW BY DEGREE

It was a simple dot on a piece of newsprint years ago. I never forgot the lesson in it.

Draw a dot on a page. This represents where you are in your life right now. Now draw a line horizontally outward to the right and place another dot on the page. This is where you will be down the road if nothing changes. This is where you will be if *you* don't change.

Now try something different. From the original starting point, shift the trajectory of the line up one degree. Now follow this line outward and upward to a new point. This is where you will be down the road if you make only a one-degree shift today. Your entire life path will be different. Instead of flatlining due to inaction, there will be movement and improvement.

The moral of the story: A small change can make a big difference. A one-degree shift today can have an exponential effect down the road. A daily affirmation, an inspirational reading, a gratitude practice, a morning prayer, a meditation—whatever it is, it's worth doing.

Instead of getting overwhelmed by the enormity of needed change, focus on incremental change in the here and now. The simplest change can change your life.

It is better to take many small steps in the right direction
than to make a great leap forward only to stumble backward.
—Chinese proverb

DAY 58
BE CURIOUS WITHOUT BEING CONSUMED

It's one thing to have healthy curiosity about people's thoughts, feelings, and behaviors. It's another thing to be consumed by them.

Being consumed is being preoccupied and overinvolved. It's a sign of poor personal boundaries. We give our power away to things over which we are powerless, and in doing so, waste precious energy.

Curiosity, on the other hand, implies detachment. It signals healthy personal boundaries and the ability to step back from others and observe. It means we know where we end and others begin.

On the road to personal freedom, we need to detach from others enough to stand in our truth and in our power. We need to take back ownership of ourselves. We have to conserve our energy and expend it productively.

Be curious. But don't be consumed.

> *Curiosity is lying in wait for every secret.*
> —Ralph Waldo Emerson

DAY 59
ACCEPT YOURSELF EXACTLY AS YOU ARE

It's one of the great paradoxes of growth and recovery. In order to change certain things about ourselves, we need to accept ourselves exactly as we are.

This is clearly a contradiction. To change, we accept what is. To create a healthier tomorrow, we plug fully into today. To become who we want to be, we embrace who we are right now.

As long as you withhold your own love and acceptance, you can't expect to grow. No one evolves in an atmosphere of blame and shame.

Think of a little child. What promotes the child's healthy development? Love, acceptance, unconditional positive regard—these are what nurture and inspire.

If there are things you want to change, that's okay. But first accept yourself exactly as you are—right here, right now.

A man cannot be comfortable without his own approval.
—Mark Twain

DAY 60
WATCH THE NOSTALGIA

Nostalgia isn't always a good thing.

Now, you might wonder what could possibly be wrong with sentimentally reminiscing about the past. It means we honor and value what was. Nostalgia is a sign of love, appreciation, and tenderheartedness.

Unfortunately, however, there's a pathological side to this coin. Nostalgia can be a sign of present discontent. We check out of today because today is uncomfortable. We glorify the past because it isn't our present. We don't like what *is*, so we yearn for what *was*.

Be careful not to discourage yourself by looking back. Watch out for telling yourself the best has come and gone—that joy is behind you. It's dangerous to think the past was when you did your best living.

It's okay to look back, but don't unplug from today. You'll never have the life you want if you check yourself out of this moment.

We seem to be going through a period of nostalgia, and everyone seems
to think yesterday was better than today. I don't think it was, and I
would advise you not to wait ten years before admitting today was
great. If you're hung up on nostalgia, pretend today is yesterday
and just go out and have one hell of a time.
—Art Buchwald

DAY 61
TAKE A MENTAL NAP

Are you an over-thinker? Do you burn so much mental fuel that you're running on empty? Is it time to give your mind a rest?

For many of us, over-thinking is an adaptation—a coping mechanism that developed in reaction to chaos and things outside our control. It's the way we adapted to circumstances that confounded and overwhelmed us.

As with any coping mechanism, this over-thinking can backfire. We burn ourselves out with all analysis. We expend precious energy trying to figure it all out.

Hyper-vigilance and over-thinking are born out of anxiety, the symptoms of something unsettled within. What's more, they don't actually alleviate the instability we feel within; they perpetuate it.

Watch that analysis paralysis. Sometimes it's best to rest that brain. It's been working overtime anyway.

Sometimes the most important thing in a whole day
is the rest we take between two deep breaths, or the
turning inwards in prayer for five short minutes.
—Etty Hillesum

DAY 62
SAY YES

Personal freedom hinges on our ability to say *yes*.

Passively resisting reality doesn't work. Resenting and feeling victimized by life circumstances only holds us hostage to them. Nothing changes if we don't first say yes. It is yes that liberates.

To say yes is to lean into our circumstances, to change what is changeable, and to let go of what's not. It means we acknowledge what's outside our control, and we do so without resentment or resistance. We accept what is in order to shape what will be.

Yes is more than a word; it's a mindset. Choose it and you will find your freedom. Say yes to it all. Say yes to your life.

God, grant me the serenity to accept the things I cannot change,
Courage to change the things I can,
And wisdom to know the difference.
—Reinhold Niebuhr

DAY 63
PUT YOUR BEST FOOT FORWARD

Accountability—to God, to the Universe, or to our own highest selves—keeps us mindful about our self-care. With a sense of accountability, we are deliberate about the steps we take. We make healthy choices. We learn and grow and try our hardest. We stretch ourselves in the ways we know we need to.

It isn't that we are performing or being artificial. It's that we feel answerable in the healthiest of ways. Instead of thinking our actions won't matter—that no one will notice anyway—we take responsibility for how we show up.

The next time you're questioning what to do, think about your "audience" and put your best foot forward. You are not an island. You are not alone. It matters how you show up.

Always do your best. What you plant now, you will harvest later.
—Og Mandino

DAY 64
LEARN FROM PAIN

When you're in the midst of darkness, does it feel like it will last forever? Do you feel powerless in the face of your pain? Do you worry you'll never feel good again? You're not alone.

Everything is temporary—every experience and every emotion. This includes pain. Keep this in mind and you will be better able to learn from your pain. You will grow through it. You will become more whole because of it.

Pain will teach you compassion and empathy. It will teach you strength and endurance. It will teach you humility, faithfulness, and perseverance. It will teach you to rely on yourself—as long as you let yourself fully experience it.

Your pain won't last forever, so learn from it while you can. You will be richer for it.

To truly laugh, you must be able to take your pain and play with it!
—Charlie Chaplin

DAY 65
HAVE A PLAN

If we don't know where we are going, we can be led just about anywhere. If we don't have our own plan, we run the risk of becoming part of someone else's. It's flat-out dangerous not to have a sense of purpose and direction.

When we don't know ourselves—when we doubt and deny our truth, or when unresolved wounding within us obscures who we are—we are susceptible to being led down all sorts of rabbit trails. Because our sense of self is weak, we allow others to tell us who we are and who to be. We become strangers to ourselves.

When we know and love ourselves, or at least when we are learning how to do so, we automatically have a plan. We have direction. We are on a journey of self-discovery—a journey to authenticity. This motivation propels us forward and keeps us on track.

Move in the direction of your true self. The forward motion will keep you from getting sidetracked. It will ward off distraction and temptation. It will keep you from becoming an actor in someone else's drama.

If you do follow your bliss you put yourself on a kind of track that has been there all the while, waiting for you, and the life that you ought to be living is the one you are living. Follow your bliss and don't be afraid, and doors will open where you didn't know they were going to be.
—Joseph Campbell

DAY 66
GET OUT OF THE HEAT

They say a frog will jump instantly out of a pot of boiling water to save itself, but it will sit in water that slowly goes from cold to hot until it cooks to death. So too can we linger in harmful situations, not realizing the heat is turning up.

Adapting to difficult circumstances can be both virtue and vice. It's good to know we can cope with adversity—that we have what it takes to get by during trying times—but we don't want to live our lives in survival mode. By tolerating the intolerable and accepting the unacceptable, we gradually abandon ourselves.

Putting up with life isn't good enough. There is a better way. Save yourself now.

Get out of the water before it gets too hot.

Each morning when I open my eyes I say to myself: I, not events, have the power to make me happy or unhappy today. I can choose which it shall be. Yesterday is dead, tomorrow hasn't arrived yet. I have just one day, today, and I'm going to be happy in it.
—Groucho Marx

DAY 67
FIGURE OUT YOUR HAPPINESS FORMULA

Each of us has our own unique formula for happiness—our own particular recipe that works just right. Our challenge is to determine what it is and follow it.

What lights you up and makes you come alive? When are you most in the "zone"? What activities cause you to lose track of time? When do you feel that wonderful sense of flow?

Pay attention to these things. Don't question them; just honor them. Give yourself permission to love what you love, free from judgment. No raining on your own parade.

Remember, people enjoy different things. What brings you pleasure is all about you. It isn't right, it isn't wrong—it's you. Discover who you are by figuring out what makes you happy.

We all have happiness habits. What are yours?

Do what makes you happy. Be with who makes you smile.
Laugh as much as you breathe, and love as long as you live.
—Author unknown

DAY 68
PRACTICE IMPERFECTIONISM

Perfectionism is nothing short of bondage.

It's an impossible standard, made up endless *shoulds*, *have tos*, and *ought tos*. It's the illusion that we have to earn our worth and value—that these can somehow be raised or lowered. It's our attempt to make up for something we see as lacking within.

Perfectionism doesn't work. It's nothing but an impossible standard. It doesn't earn us worth and value; rather, it holds us hostage, wears us down, and keeps us disillusioned.

Be loving, graceful, and forgiving with yourself. Try loosening up, lightening up, and letting go. Practice imperfectionism.

Stop fighting your humanness and lean into it. Embrace your perfect imperfection. It will be truly liberating.

You're not lovable in spite of your humanity. You're lovable because of it!

Gold cannot be pure, and people cannot be perfect.
—Chinese proverb

DAY 69
DEMAND RESPECT

Make sure the people in your life treat you well.

At face value, this might sound unrealistic, even egotistical. Who are we to make anyone treat us a certain way? But this isn't about making anyone do anything. This is not about controlling or demanding. It has nothing to do with changing other people.

This is about surrounding yourself with people who treat you the way you deserve to be treated. It's about attracting respectful behavior from others. It's about confronting what is inappropriate and stepping away from unhealthy dynamics. It's about taking care of yourself.

When we take care of ourselves with others—when we insist on healthy dynamics—our relationships feed us and fuel us. We feel buoyed, supported, and nurtured. We experience a wonderful synergy within our relationships. Our dynamics energize rather than drain us as toxic relationships tend to do.

You have the power to ensure—or at least profoundly increase the likelihood—that the people in your inner circle, without exception, treat you well.

If you want to be respected by others the great thing is to respect yourself.
Only by that, only by self-respect will you compel others to respect you.
—Fyodor Dostoyevsky

DAY 70
BE HUMAN

"I'm human." I just love saying it.

Too often we package ourselves up, box ourselves in, and deny our humanness. We have this expectation that life is meant to be comfortable, that things are meant to go smoothly, and that we are supposed to be perfect. These expectations do nothing but drag us down.

When exactly did we disconnect from our humanness? Where along the way did we learn to hold our breath, hoping upon hope we wouldn't make a mistake and reveal our imperfection? When did we learn to perform, rather than just be?

Your job isn't to perform. It isn't to do everything right. It isn't to be perfect. Your job is to be human. It's to be who you are and to make the mistakes we all make in order to learn.

Stop expecting things to be so tidy. Being human is anything but.

Imperfection clings to a person, and if they wait till they are brushed off entirely, they would spin for ever on their axis, advancing nowhere.
—*Thomas Carlyle*

DAY 71
CELEBRATE THE BLANK SLATE

If we come into the world a blank slate to be written upon, and if our world wrote upon us some negative things along the way, we have the power to edit the script. We get to rewrite the parts that don't work for us.

English philosopher John Locke put forth the theory of "tabula rasa" (blank slate). We are born free and clear. We are born blank slates. Everything we know today comes from our environment, from our experiences, and from our perceptions of these experiences.

As we move through life, we gather information, create thoughts, and form beliefs. Our slate gets written upon. Early on, we didn't have much of a say in what was written. We were powerless over many of our thoughts and beliefs. But we need not be powerless anymore.

It is possible to clear the slate and begin again. As adults, we get to choose our inner dialogue, our thoughts, and our beliefs.

Examine what you have been told. Reject what doesn't work for you. Make the most of the blank slate by writing on it what you choose.

If you don't change your beliefs,
your life will be like this forever. Is that good news?
—William Somerset Maugham

DAY 72
BE WHO YOU CHOOSE TO BE

Do you live your life in competition and comparison? Do you base your sense of self on how the world is treating you or on how you measure up? Are you living in a state of perpetual reaction?

There is no peace or freedom in reactivity. If your sense of self is up for debate, you will find reasons around every corner to feel persecuted and judged. You will find evidence for feeling one up or one down, better than or less than. Your identity will be fragile and temperamental.

You need not look to your world to tell you who you are. Your true identity is far more enduring than that. Your worth and value are not up for debate. Your sense of self isn't in the hands of others.

It was never between you and them anyway.

Don't let the negativity given to you by the world disempower you.
Instead give to yourself that which empowers you.
—Les Brown

DAY 73
BE DETERMINED

If we want a new life, we have to wake up to how we might be perpetuating harmful themes from our past. We need to take responsibility for how we are treating ourselves. We have to open our eyes, get a little outraged, and proclaim, "No more!"

Channel that healthy indignation into loving and honoring yourself. Break free from old thinking. Reject unhealthy patterns. Liberate yourself from yesterday.

If you're tired of putting up with the status quo, become adamant about changing it. Perhaps it's time you were a little fed up.

It's not who you are that holds you back; it's who you think you're not.
—Author unknown

DAY 74
CHOOSE NON-REACTION

Do you mirror other people's behaviors? Do you tend to match inappropriate conduct with more of the same? If someone wrongs you, do you wrong them back?

Perhaps you recognize this tendency in yourself and its a pattern you want to break. Or maybe you're not quite sure you want to break it. You might think that doing to others some of what they've done to you is the more powerful position. It isn't. This kind of reactivity is always the weaker position.

On the other hand, there's nothing weak about choosing nonreaction. There's nothing soft about standing in your integrity and making a decision not to match others people's behavior. Choosing not to react isn't letting others off the hook.

It takes strength to stand in your truth, to be true to yourself, and to hold your power rather than give it away. It takes courage to respond rather than react.

There's nothing weak about it.

Everything can be taken from a man but one thing:
the last of human freedoms—the ability to choose one's
attitude in any given set of circumstances, to choose one's way.
—Viktor Frankl

DAY 75
TAKE BACK YOUR WORTH AND VALUE

We all make mistakes. We all fall from grace. We hurt ourselves. We hurt others. We disappoint. We fail. None of this is who we are; it's what we do.

You are not your actions; you are the actor. Your behaviors might be good or bad—this doesn't mean you are good or bad.

You came into this world worthy and valuable. You came into this world lovable and deserving of love. Nothing you do or don't do can take this away from you.

If you confuse your worth and value with your behaviors, your sense of self will be up then down, strong then weak. You will fight your humanness. You will try to earn your value by telling yourself you have to be good—always.

To love yourself—to open yourself to growth—is to make one critical distinction. It's the distinction between your behaviors and your worth and value.

Go ahead. Own your behaviors. Just take back your worth and value from them.

You cannot solve a problem from the same consciousness that created it.
You must learn to see the world anew.
—Albert Einstein

DAY 76
SEE WHAT IGNITES YOU

Each of us has a spirit that wants to be ignited, a life force longing to be activated—one that calls us to action.

But are we answering the call? Or do we judge what we love and disapprove of our passions? Do we tell ourselves they are not grand enough, worthy enough, or significant enough to matter?

As hard as you may try to discourage yourself, your spirit simply won't be ignored. You have a powerful life force within you. You can disregard it, but it will speak up and make itself known. The question is, will you act on it?

It's your birthright to be passionate. Claim this passion by noticing what lights you up. Pay attention to your enthusiasm level as you move through your day. See what energizes and inspires you. Where does your life force call you to go?

Be a bright light. Get ignited. You deserve it. The world deserves it.

Like what you do. If you don't like it, do something else.
—Paul Harvey

DAY 77
PUT YOUR ENERGY WHERE YOUR POWER IS

We tend to ruminate over the past. We fret about the future. We preoccupy ourselves with how others show up. We are confounded by the world around us, expending our energy on things outside our control. We step out of our power and disconnect from our core.

The only person you control is *you*. The only thoughts, feelings, and behaviors over which you have authority are your own. The only time in which you have true power is now. You are in charge of your reality. And you can take back sovereignty over yourself at any time.

When you find yourself spinning out—when your energy feels diffused and scattered and you're giving yourself over to anything that takes you away from *you*—bring yourself back home. Ground yourself in your power again. Reclaim what you've been giving away.

Life can render us powerless in an instant. The good news is we can step back into our power at any time.

He who controls others may be powerful,
but he who has mastered himself is mightier still.
—Lao Tzu

DAY 78
PRAY

We need to show up for ourselves. We need to be proactive about creating lives we love. We need to take a hands-on approach to our wellness—mind, body, and spirit. At the same time, we must not turn our backs on spirituality and inspiration.

Take charge of your life—and pray to the source from which you derive strength, courage, and hope. Be self-sufficient—and seek support. Find power within yourself—and find it in a power greater than yourself. It's a synergistic partnership. It's a working relationship.

Grow yourself. Rely on yourself. Come to your own assistance. And all the while, pray.

Pray as though everything depended on God.
Work as though everything depended on you.
—Saint Augustine

DAY 79
MAKE PEACE WITH NOT KNOWING

The why's of life—and our fierce attachment to them—can be our downfall. We tell ourselves we need to make sense of everything. We need to understand all that's unknown. The truth is, mystery surpasses understanding. That's what makes it mystery.

Let go of that compulsive, often obsessive need to figure it all out. Open yourself to the wonder of the unknown. Make peace with not knowing.

The mystery of life holds riches for us. The mystery of life keeps us curious, humble, and intrigued.

Some things are simply beyond comprehension. It's a wonderful thing.

As I make my slow pilgrimage through the world,
a certain sense of beautiful mystery seems to gather and grow.
—A. C. Benson

DAY 80
WALK OUT OF YOUR HISTORY

There comes a time when we can't ignore ourselves any longer—when we have to make a decision to become the person we want to become, not who our histories said we were.

The past will box us in if we let it. Old identities and outdated beliefs hold us back from stepping into the fullness of who we are. We get stuck in what was. We miss out on what will be.

Your past is not your potential, and today is a new day. Break out of the status quo. Reinvent yourself. Be the person you want to become. Claim your life.

Step out of your past so you can become your future.

However long the night, the dawn will break.
—African proverb

DAY 81
LISTEN TO YOURSELF

Do you shame, blame, and judge yourself? Do treat yourself worse than you would ever treat another? Are you pretty ruthless about it? Well, STOP. Your subconscious is listening.

Maybe all you've ever known is criticism and condemnation. Maybe it's sheer habit. But it isn't okay. That little kid inside of you—that precious and worthy *you* within—is acutely aware of what you're saying and the messages you're sending.

I ache as I reflect on the cruelties uttered to myself over the years. I also rejoice in the awareness it won't happen again. At the very least, I'll catch myself in the act and redirect my thinking.

Take responsibility for how you treat yourself. Witness the thinker within you, and listen to the self-talk. Be more conscientious about what you're saying.

Your subconscious is listening.

He who would be useful, strong, and happy must cease to be a passive receptacle for the negative, beggarly, and impure streams of thought; and as a wise householder commands his servants and invites his guests, so must he learn to command his desires and to say, with authority, what thoughts he shall admit into the mansion of his soul.
—James Allen

DAY 82
LEARN SOMETHING NEW

Please stop faulting yourself for thinking what you think, believing what you believe, and feeling what you feel. It all makes sense. You learned what you lived.

We are products of our histories, profoundly shaped by early life experiences. We are molded by how we were treated and by the messages we received, whether overtly or covertly, explicitly or implicitly. Acknowledging what we learned along the way and how it has affected us is essential.

This isn't about blame and shame. It isn't about blaming our past or shaming ourselves for carrying on the themes of the past. It's about gaining insight in order to break free.

Awareness is the pathway to change. Awareness of your past will lead to acceptance of yourself and how you have perhaps perpetuated patterns from your history. All of this will propel action as you show up for yourself in a whole new way.

You are a product of your environment. You are a product of so much you did not choose. Today, however, you have a choice.

Not everything that is faced can be changed.
But nothing can be changed until it is faced.
—James Baldwin

DAY 83
HAVE A WISH FOR YOURSELF

What do you wish for? How often do you think about it?

It's important to have something for which you hunger. Call it a dream, a hope, a wish. It isn't necessarily pie in the sky—just a basic desire for yourself and your life.

Perhaps it's laughter and joy. Perhaps it's friendship and family. Maybe you wish for confidence and empowerment, patience, or faith.

A wish keeps you growing, seeking, and aspiring for something. A parent has a wish for his or her child, and you need to have a wish for yourself. It's your vision. It's your hope.

My wish for you is that you have a wish for yourself.

You are never too old to set another goal or to dream a new dream.
—C. S. Lewis

DAY 84
GET OUT OF YOUR WAY

We blame all sorts of things for our lack of progress. We blame others. We blame circumstance. We blame our histories. We even blame the passage of time. The truth is, we are often our greatest obstacles.

By unwittingly allowing old thoughts, emotions, and personal limitations to impede forward movement, we limit our growth. Out of habit, we hold ourselves back. We create our own roadblocks by continuing to invite the past into the present.

What if you removed yourself as your greatest impediment? What if you allowed the positive energy within you to flow?

Before you achieve anything, you have to get out of your own way.

Everything in the universe is within you. Ask all from yourself.
—Rumi

DAY 85
FILL UP THE TANK, PUMP UP THE TIRE, AND KEEP GOING

Let's say you headed out on a cross-country road trip and mid-journey you ran out of gas or got a flat tire. What would you do? Would you throw in the towel and head home? No. You would fill up the tank or pump up the tire and keep going.

The way you look at the bumps in the road says a lot about whether you let yourself be human, whether you work your way through setbacks, and whether you believe you are worth the effort of continuing on. Think about it.

When you hit a roadblock in your journey, the best idea is to always fill up the tank, pump up the tires, and keep on going.

Nobody trips over mountains. It is the small pebble that causes you to stumble. Pass all the pebbles in your path and you will find you have crossed the mountain.
—Author unknown

DAY 86
DETACH

Look at the things you have been clinging to because you tell yourself they offer you security. Now consider the fact that this security is an illusion.

No person, place, or thing can give you the kind of refuge you can only find deep within. It's actually an inside job.

If we feel weak and vulnerable, it is natural to grasp at things outside of us to feel secure. It is understandable why we would attach to anything and everything in order to feel whole. But this coping pattern backfires.

The attachments we form suppress us and stifle our life force. They hold us hostage. They lock all insecurity within and keep us from evolving. True security is about letting go of our attachments and relying on ourselves to feel complete. Our sanctuary is within.

Let go of the illusion of security. Give up the false gods. Set yourself free.

The man who looks for security, even in the mind, is like a man who would chop off his limbs in order to have artificial ones which will give him no pain or trouble.
—Henry Miller

DAY 87
CONFIRM THE POSITIVE BIAS

Our beliefs want to be proven right. They always find a way of doing so.

In other words, it's a natural human tendency. We gravitate toward, and favor, any data that confirms the fundamental biases we hold. We collect and remember information selectively. We interpret life experiences in a slanted way. This principle applies to the biases we hold about ourselves as well.

If our beliefs about ourselves are negative, they will be proven correct. We gather, knowingly or unknowingly, any and all information that supports these negative core beliefs. As we collect our evidence, our negative beliefs often grow stronger. We become further convinced of our own unworthiness.

Shift your bias about yourself, and your entire life experience will shift. Start telling yourself positive things about who you are, and get busy validating them. You shouldn't have any trouble finding supporting evidence!

Over time, your new thoughts will become beliefs. You'll see the truth of who you are—and who you have always been. You will find the world sees it too.

Watch those beliefs. They will be proven right.

We do not see things as they are. We see them as we are.
—Talmud

DAY 88
CHANGE THE WAY YOU LOOK AT THE UNKNOWN

We often freeze in the face of the unknown. Like deer in headlights, we feel immobilized by uncertainty. It need not be so scary.

Life is full of uncertainty. How we experience it has everything to do with attitude. We can look at uncertainty from the perspective of a child or an adult, from a place of disempowerment or empowerment, in a spirit of inaction or action.

As we look to our future, we naturally conjure up all sorts of *what ifs*. But what's the nature of our what ifs? The functional, empowered adult doesn't attatch fear and negativity to the unknown, but sees it as simply that—unknown. It isn't bad; it isn't good.

Your healthiest self knows that whatever comes to pass, you will meet yourself in that place—and you will be okay. You accept mystery in life. At the same time, you know you have the power to shape your future. You understand that you contribute to your own positive outcomes by showing up for yourself in the now—one empowered today at a time.

You are anything but helpless when it comes to your future. You need not freeze up in the face of the unkown. Lean into it. Embrace it. You have the power to shape what will be.

I need neither future nor past, but to learn to take today not too fast.
—Jeb Dickerson

DAY 89
BE YOUR OWN WORK IN PROGRESS

"I'm a work in progress." I just love how it feels.

Always be on the lookout for how you can become stronger, wiser, deeper, and more spiritual. Look at every life experience in terms of what you can take away from it and how you can give back to your world a more enlightened person.

It's okay to be a work in progress. In fact, it's unavoidable. From birth to death, we are growing and changing. But not everyone sinks their teeth into this process. Not everyone embraces personal growth. This is where choice comes in.

Get passionate about your evolution. Be your own work in progress. Whatever you do, keep working on you.

It takes a deep commitment to change
and an even deeper commitment to grow.
—Ralph Ellison

DAY 90
BE DISCERNING

If you want to live a life you love, you need to be selective about what you do and do not invite into it, about the people you do and do not engage with, and about where you do and do not devote your energy.

We may not have had a say about our environments early on, about what influenced us, and about the forces that acted upon us each day, but as adults we *do* have a say. And we have a responsibility to create for ourselves an environment that supports a healthy, satisfying existence.

To live a truly liberated life you have to be discriminating about every aspect of it. So get choosy. Give yourself permission to shape your life as you wish.

If you aren't discerning about your life, who will be?

The secret of health for both mind and body is not to mourn
for the past, worry about the future, or anticipate troubles,
but to live in the present moment wisely and earnestly.
—Buddha

DAY 91
ACT THE WAY YOU WANT TO FEEL

If you want feel a certain way, act that way. If you want to feel happy, act happy. If you want to feel grateful, act grateful. If you want to feel passionate, be passionate. If you want to feel satisfied, do things that satisfy. If you want to be excited about life, then do what it takes to get excited about life!

Waiting around for our thoughts and feelings to change before we take action keeps us on hold and puts off how we want to experience life. Sometimes we simply need to take action. We need to act our way into a new reality.

Live the outcomes you want. Be productive. Accomplish goals. Express gratitude. Pursue your dreams. Do things you love.

If you don't like how you're feeling, show up differently. Be the solution you seek. One action at a time you will shift the way you feel about yourself and your life.

How do *you* want to feel? And how can you act your way into that place?

Be the change you wish to see in the world.
—Mahatma Gandhi

DAY 92
WATCH THE SELF-LABELING

Many of us cling to negative identities. These labels we wear on the inside constrict and constrain. They don't serve us, but we hold on to them.

Especially harmful are the labels we give ourselves based on some former self or past experience. "I'm a chronic underachiever." "I'm needy." "I'm negative." "I'm a follower, not a leader." "I'm a glass half empty person." "I'm just a dreamer." "I can't do anything right." "I will never change."

We stereotype ourselves. We possess a tendency—or possessed one at one time—and it becomes our identity, taking on a life of its own. We perpetuate our labels, and in so doing, make no room whatsoever for growth and change. We overgeneralize. We lock ourselves in.

If you're wearing negative labels and you want to break free from them, try proving and disproving them. Challenge yourself to find evidence that the labels fit. Then look for evidence to the contrary. If you try to disprove an absolute, which is what our labels usually are, you will always be able to do so.

Outgrow your labels. You decide who you are. No label gets to decide for you.

Madness is a preference for the symbol over that which it represents.
—G. K. Chesterton

DAY 93
TAKE OFF THE MASKS

We play many roles in this life. Whether it's mother, father, husband, wife, son, daughter, boss, employee, student, or any other role, each of us wears many hats. Needless to say, there's nothing intrinsically wrong with this.

The danger comes when we role-play ourselves. By wearing certain masks in order to be lovable—by putting on a game face in order to be well received—we risk our personal freedom.

If you know and accept who you are at your core and you happen to play many roles in life, there's no problem. If you create a role and call it you, all because you have no idea who you are at your core, something has to change.

Go ahead. Role-play. Just don't role-play *you*.

> *We get so much in the habit of wearing disguises before others that we finally appear disguised before ourselves.*
> —Francois de la Rochefoucauld

DAY 94
SEEK INTERDEPENDENCE

In the world of relationships, we speak of dependence, independence, and interdependence. Only one of these fosters strong and satisfying relationships. On the road to personal freedom, interdependence is the way to go.

Dependence is a reactive posture, one in which we overidentify with others, allow ourselves to be excessively vulnerable, and tend to feel victimized because of it. We lose ourselves to our relationships. Independence is another reactive posture, but one in which we wall off, hold back, and feel disconnected as a result. We cling fiercely to self within our relationships.

With interdependence, we know who we are, we are in charge of our realities, and we relate to others with self-awareness. We maintain healthy boundaries. We protect ourselves and at the same time, allow ourselves be vulnerable. We are conscious and discerning about how we show up. We know that intimacy and autonomy are not mutually exclusive. We strike a balance in our relationships. We maintain self with others.

If you've been relating to others more reactively than intentionally, it's time for rebalancing. It's time for interdependence.

Relationships are the hallmark of the mature person.
—Brian Tracy

DAY 95
PUT YOURSELF IN A BUBBLE

Boundaries are a regular topic in our home. A day rarely passes without mention of the "bubble."

Your bubble is your happy place and safe space. It's where you feel secure and buffered. It's the zone in which you feel at peace. It's where you are self-preserved and self-determined.

Your boundaries are your bubble. They are the personal limits that define, protect, and contain you. They give you the right of discernment about what you take in and leave out. You will need boundaries in order to have any kind of stability of self and to maintain consistency in your internal experience.

Think about the state of your personal boundaries. If they are weak, shore them up. Then make sure you uphold them. You control and maintain your bubble. No one else will, and no one else can. It's up to you to preserve your peace.

Go ahead—put yourself in a bubble. Just make sure to invite in what makes you happy.

Self-preservation is the first law of nature.
—Samuel Butler

DAY 96
ALLOW YOURSELF TO DESERVE

There is no one more deserving than you.

It's a bold statement. But bold as it may sound, it's 100 percent true. How this kind of statement hits us speaks volumes about our relationship with ourselves.

Many of us think we got shortchanged in the worth and value department. We see worth and value in others, but we don't see them in ourselves. If we ever had them, they must have been lost along the way.

The truth is, each of us comes into the world deserving. Each of us is inherently worthy and valuable. These qualities can't be raised or lowered—they simply are. They are our birthright. They're not up for measurement or comparison. They're not up for debate.

Go ahead—boldly proclaim, "There's no one more deserving than I am," or "No one has more worth and value than I do." Don't be sheepish about it.

You can search throughout the entire universe for someone who is
more deserving of your love and affection than you are yourself,
and that person is not to be found anywhere. You yourself, as much
as anybody in the entire universe deserve your love and affection.
—Buddha

DAY 97
MAKE ROOM FOR MISTAKES

If you're someone who doesn't allow for your own imperfection, it's time to look at your relationship with guilt.

Guilt can be healthy or toxic. Healthy guilt is important. It gives us direction. It tells us about ourselves and our value system. It's the emotion we feel because we have acted against our core beliefs and values. Healthy guilt doesn't diminish us or our sense of inherent worth. It helps us correct ourselves when need be.

Toxic guilt, however, is a remnant of dysfunction. It's something we came to feel because of unhealthy circumstances. It's an inflated sense of responsibility, and it allows no room for mistakes. We feel rigid and overwhelmed. We think we have to be perfect in order to be lovable.

Look at your relationship with guilt. Clean it up if you need to. There is no room for making no room for mistakes!

A diamond with a flaw is worth more
than a pebble without imperfections.
—Chinese proverb

DAY 98
EXTERNALIZE YOUR REALITY

We can't heal what we don't acknowledge. This means we can't heal pain if we don't recognize it. And if we don't heal our pain, we will never be free.

Pain kept within grows and worsens with time, touching every aspect of who we are. There is also a compounding effect with pain. Left unexpressed and unhealed, it simply begets more pain, negatively influencing how we experience our world.

If you have been stuffing pain, it's time to let it out. Find a healthy outlet. Talk about it. Write about it. Direct that emotional energy in a new direction.

Get current with what you feel so you can be fully available to life.

The truth that many people never understand, until it is too late,
is that the more you try to avoid suffering, the more you suffer,
because smaller and more insignificant things begin to torture
you in proportion to your fear of being hurt.
—Thomas Merton

DAY 99
HAVE FAITH

Time gives us the gift of perspective. With the passage of time, we come to see all we have gained through our troubles, the growth that has come from hardship, and the importance of it all. We come to value our human experience in all its forms.

Just because you can't fathom the purpose in your pain doesn't mean there isn't one. It's hard to find significance in suffering, especially in the midst of it, but if you look for it you will find it. In time, you will uncover the meaning.

Pain offers us the opportunity to grow stronger. It challenges us to dig deep and evolve. It enriches and softens us. It gives us wisdom, humility, and humanity. It connects us with the human family.

Fear not. You need not understand it all right now. Just keep moving forward. Keep walking through the pain. The meaning will become clear.

Life can only be understood backwards; but it must be lived forwards.
—Soren Kierkegaard

DAY 100
LEARN THE GOOD LIFE

The good life isn't something you just have. It isn't a matter of luck. It isn't a matter of fate. And you don't have to be born into it. In many ways, the good life is a learned experience. You too can learn it.

Whatever your circumstances, whatever your history, and whatever your limitations or disadvantages, past or present, you can learn to embrace all that's good in your life. You can learn to celebrate who you are, soar with your strengths, and maximize all that's within you.

The good life isn't out there somewhere. It's within you, waiting to be actualized.

To do so, you might have to look at how you define the good life. You might have to undo some misconceptions. You might have to push through some resentments and feelings of deprivation.

It's not the circumstances you've been given—it's what you make of them.

I am still determined to be cheerful and happy, in whatever situation
I may be; for I have also learned from experience that the greater
part of our happiness or misery depends upon our dispositions,
and not upon our circumstances.
—Martha Washington

DAY 101
GO AGAINST YOUR INSTINCTS SOMETIMES

There is a wonderful *Seinfeld* episode in which George turns his entire life around by going completely against his instincts. It might be time for you to do the same.

Instead of continuing to lie to women out of fear of rejection, he says, "My name is George, I'm unemployed, and I live with my parents." He lands himself a beautiful girlfriend. She then gets him an interview with the Yankees.

At the interview, instead of his typical sycophancy, he gives Steinbrenner a piece of his mind. "In the past twenty years, you have caused myself [sic] and the city of New York a good deal of distress, as we have watched you take our beloved Yankees and reduce them to a laughingstock, all for the glorification of your massive ego." Steinbrenner hires him on the spot.

If your instincts, like George's, have not been serving you well, a self-defeating internal dialogue might be to blame. Instincts can't always be trusted—not if they're born out of dysfunction and insecurity.

If your decision-making has been leading you astray, challenge the mindset behind it. Go against the grain. Your life might change for the better.

I do not believe in a fate that falls on men however they act;
but I do believe in a fate that falls on man unless they act.
—G. K. Chesterton

DAY 102
WATCH THE SEMANTICS

Life is a choice, not a chore. But many of us make it sound as if life is a job we have to do, where everything within is a job duty. We see pressure and obligation where we might otherwise see freedom and empowerment. It could be a matter of semantics.

Notice the general vibe of what you say. Is there a lot of "have to," "need to," "should," and "can't" in your repertoire? What if you shifted to "want to," "choose to," "will," and "can"?

"I need to go to the gym today" becomes "I will get some exercise today."

"I should really do my affirmations" becomes "I want to work on my positive self-talk."

Chores can become what you choose. It's all in the attitude. And since you speak your attitude, watch your semantics. Choose the language of freedom.

Life can be hard when you "have to." It's much easier when you "want to."

No one saves us but ourselves. No one can and no one may.
We ourselves must walk the path.
—Buddha

DAY 103
DETACH FROM WHAT ISN'T YOURS

Do you feel like you're carrying the weight of the world on your shoulders? Do you make a habit of assuming other people's problems? Do you feel like you don't have a choice?

On our path to personal freedom, we need to figure out what is and isn't ours. We need to see where we end and where others begin. We need to acknowledge the price we have paid for carrying what doesn't belong to us. We need to see how we have gotten lost in the shuffle.

This isn't about divorcing yourself from empathy and compassion. It isn't about being selfish and heartless. It's about recognizing the difference between caregiving and caretaking.

Caregiving is doing for others what they cannot do for themselves. Caretaking is doing for others what they *can* do. The former is selfless in the healthiest of ways. The latter is selfless in an enmeshed, self-abandoning kind of way.

It's okay not to carry other people's burdens. It's okay to detach. It might feel as if you're breaking the rules, but detach anyway. It's very liberating.

He who would be serene and pure needs but one thing: detachment.
—Meister Eckhart

DAY 104
CONFRONT THE DARK AND LET THE LIGHT IN

If we wish to be free, then honest self-examination is a must. To live a life of integrity, we need to confront who we are. As long as we lock parts of ourselves away, hiding them lest we be revealed as bad or unworthy, we cannot live a liberated life.

You don't have to hide who you are, and you need not deny the darkness. It's part of your humanness. Denying it only closes you off. In suppressing your true self, you block your ability to receive.

Look straight at yourself instead. Embrace all of who you are. Forgive yourself where needed. Commit yourself to working with your weaknesses and soaring with your strengths. Look at the darkness, and celebrate the light.

Make the most of who you are.

Confront the dark parts of yourself, and work to banish them with
illumination and forgiveness. Your willingness to wrestle with
your demons will cause your angels to sing. Use the pain
as fuel, as a reminder of your strength.
—August Wilson

DAY 105
LOOK, LEARN, AND LET GO

We tend to approach our histories in one of two ways. Some of us say to ourselves, "It is what it is," and "Just get over it." Some of us get stuck in the past, dwelling on it and feeling victimized by it all.

Neither of these approaches works. Thankfully, however, they're not our only options. There is another way.

First, look right at your history. Turn toward it and shine a realistic and honest light upon it all. Accept your history as part of your life story.

Next, learn from your history. Identify the lessons along the way. How has your past been your teacher? How has it challenged you and helped you to grow? In what ways are you richer for it?

Lastly, when you have acknowledged, accepted, and learned something from your history, it's time to let go.

It would be asking the impossible of yourself to simply let go without fully coming to terms with your past and naming the lessons in it. It's also impossible to let go if you're stuck in a victim position. But when you can say with confidence that you accept your history and are better off for it, then you can let go.

You can make peace with your past. Just look at it, learn from it, and let it go.

Learn the past, watch the present, and create the future.
—Author unknown

DAY 106
CHANGE WHAT YOU CAN

Nothing frustrates like trying to control the uncontrollables. We resist the truth that certain things are outside our power. We try to claim power over them, and we end up feeling frustrated and helpless.

Scratch the surface of this kind of control and you'll find fear. The need to be in control is an adaptation to anxiety and instability within. It's how we believed we could manage our fear. If we could control our environments, we thought, we would feel okay inside.

But control is an illusion. Trying to control what you are incapable of controlling only keeps you trapped in a cycle of fear and futility. It doesn't work.

Free yourself. Buy yourself some peace by acknowledging and accepting what is beyond your control.

Let go of what you can't change. Then change what you can.

Happiness and freedom begin with a clear understanding of one principle: some things are within our control and some things are not. It is only after you have faced up to this fundamental rule and learned to distinguish between what you can and cannot control that inner tranquility and outer effectiveness become possible.
—Epictetus

DAY 107
AD-LIB YOUR LIFE

If you've been living life by a script that doesn't serve you, it's time for a rewrite.

You know the old script by heart. You've been repeating the lines for years. But just because you've memorized them doesn't mean they're a fit. There's a good chance it's not even the right script—and never was.

Many people have contributed to your internal dialogue—all sorts of voices from your past. Some of their messages have served you. Encouraging and affirming, these lines from your life script have helped you know and love yourself.

Some of the messages haven't served you at all. They have helped form a belief system that's anything but liberating—and the messages have been playing out in your subconscious ever since.

Negative thoughts keep you stuck in old behavior patterns. They sabotage your efforts at a better life. They're familiar—even comfortable—but they've been holding you back.

Be bold. Toss out the script. It's time to ad-lib a little!

Courage is the power to let go of the familiar.
—Raymond Lindquist

DAY 108
FACE YOURSELF

We expend precious energy coping, surviving, and running from ourselves. We drain our life force trying to be who we are not, escaping the discomfort of our own reality. Perhaps it's what we have always done.

But what if you did an about-face? What if you met yourself head-on instead? What would happen then?

Getting honest with yourself is always preferable to a life of escape. What you find might be painful and overwhelming. It might be uncomfortable and difficult to accept. But you can't heal what you don't acknowledge. If you want a liberated life, honesty is a must.

Turn and face yourself. It isn't as scary as you think. You can't outrun yourself forever.

Be patient toward all that is unsolved in your heart, and try to love the questions themselves like locked rooms and like books that are written in a very foreign tongue. Do not now seek the answers, which cannot be given you because you would not be able to live them. And the point is, to live everything. Live the questions now. Perhaps you will find them gradually, without noticing it, and live along some distant day into the answer.
—Rainer Maria Rilke

DAY 109
CLEAR AWAY THE CLUTTER

Emotional clutter clouds our perspective and impedes our growth. It weighs us down and drains our life force. It sabotages our chances for happiness.

Many of us have emotional clutter. It's made up of past hurts, unresolved wounds, and painful emotional memories. It's the burden of negative core beliefs and the yoke of a painful self-image. Freedom hinges on our ability to clear this clutter.

To do so, you will need to expose your emotional clutter, trace its origins, and uncover the messages perpetuating your emotional stuckness. You will need to reveal the stories you've been telling yourself and the lies by which you have been living. You will need to be committed to the work of freeing yourself from a painful history.

Clear away that clutter. Your happiness depends on it.

We do not receive wisdom; we must discover it for ourselves after a journey through the wilderness, which no one else can make for us, which no one can spare us, for our wisdom is the point of view from which we come at last to regard the world.
—Marcel Proust

DAY 110
SEEK UNDERSTANDING

Your life is a sacred journey to authenticity—a voyage to true self. In many ways, it's your labyrinth.

The labyrinth is an ancient symbol used in meditation and prayer. It represents a journey to our core and the subsequent journey back out into our world. In the labyrinth, we go to the center of our being, we gain insight along the way, and we reengage in our world with new-found awareness and authenticity. Interestingly enough, the way into the labyrinth is the way out.

We seekers know our journey works this way. We seek knowledge. We search for understanding. With honesty and humility, we journey within. We look at and learn about ourselves. We bring to our lives heightened understanding. We experience the world increasingly genuinely. Life gets richer.

Go on an expedition. Journey to your core. Seek understanding. Engage in your life in a whole new way. The way in is the way out.

What you seek is seeking you.
—Rumi

DAY 111
QUESTION EVERYTHING

The day comes when we start asking questions. If we want to live authentic, empowered lives, we muster up courage, stop blindly accepting, and get curious about who we are at our core.

To rely on others to tell you who you are is to relinquish your power. To accept a course others have charted for you is to be a follower. To adopt what the world says about you is to put your identity in the hands of everyone but the one person in whose hands it should be.

Don't let your identity be co-opted. Accept no one's opinion as your own. Question it all.

Learn from yesterday, live for today, hope for tomorrow.
The important thing is not to stop questioning.
—Albert Einstein

DAY 112
PRESERVE YOUR HAPPY PLACE

Your happy place is the space in which you feel secure, serene, and self-defined. It's where you feel inspired and motivated. It's where you feel most like *you*. Your happy place is a mental, emotional, physical, and spiritual construct. Only you can define it. Only you get to protect and preserve it.

Think about what helps you feel peaceful and contented. Art, music, a beautiful environment…these could be some such things. Surround yourself with them. Think about what helps you maintain conscious contact with your higher power. Meditation, prayer, spending time in nature…these could be some such practices. Engage in them. Think about what helps you feel optimistic and encouraged. Positive images, visual reminders, affirmations…these are but a few. Nurture yourself with them.

Each of us gets to create—and continuously re-create—our own happy place. In so doing, we protect what we cherish.

There are some days when I think I am going
to die from an overdose of satisfaction.
—Salvador Dali

DAY 113
LEAVE AND LEARN

Leaving isn't necessarily giving up or running away. In leaving there can be learning. In leaving there can be profound gain. In leaving we often find freedom.

On our journey to personal freedom, we do a lot of stripping away. We do a lot of leaving. This signals movement. It says we are stepping out of old roles and rules. It means we are shedding the inauthentic and revealing what's true. It says we are graduating from what was, so as to step into what will be.

We leave relationships that aren't working, jobs that are an ill fit, and situations that are unhealthy. We leave our childhoods and the baggage of our wounding. We leave behind old self-conceptions, entering into more loving relationships with ourselves.

Keep learning and evolving. Let your growth chart your course through life. Let your healing steer the way. As you do, much will be left behind. This is a good thing.

We have to let go of the old to grab onto the new.

Letting go doesn't mean giving up...it means moving on.
—Author unknown

DAY 114
HEAL WITH GRATITUDE

We all have turmoil. We all have loss. We all have grief. It's part of the human experience. It's that unwelcome intruder in our human journey.

But it need not color the whole of our existence. Managed well, we can move through grief without it becoming a chronic condition.

Try healing grief with gratitude. Look at the painful experiences in your life. Now find the gratitude. It might be gratitude for insight and wisdom—for the chance to learn and grow. Maybe there is a spiritual lesson you learned. Perhaps you see how grief has made you richer and more complete.

Following my mother's death, the most profound and painful loss I'd experienced, gratitude was literally my lifesaver. Gratitude focused me. Gratitude gave me hope. Gratitude cloaked me in a kind of serenity and spirituality.

Look for the blessings in even the most painful circumstances. By doing so, you'll be more likely to accept and move through them. You'll find you come out the other side better off for having had them. Even in the depths of despair, you can find something for which to feel grateful.

Give yourself the comfort and healing you deserve. Do it with gratitude.

Gratitude is heaven itself.
—William Blake

DAY 115
DIG A NEW GROOVE

Dysfunctional patterns don't develop overnight. Nor do functional ones.

It takes time to dig well-worn grooves of patterned behavior. If you want to carve out a healthier life path and break patterns that are not serving you, you will need to start digging a new groove.

Commit yourself to creating something new. Practice new behaviors. Be diligent about your new path. Consistent right action, along with the commitment to intercede on yourself when appropriate, will keep you from recreating old patterns and slipping back into that familiar status quo.

While it takes time to dig a new groove, fear not. It takes less time to dig a healthy groove than it took to dig the unhealthy one. So start today. Before you know it, you will have created a whole new normal.

Motivation is what gets you started. Habit is what keeps you going.
—Jim Rohn

DAY 116
CREATE A LIFE HANDBOOK

Wouldn't it be great if life came with instructions? Couldn't we all benefit from a manual? Go ahead—create one. Design your own life handbook.

Within it will be the nuts and bolts of your journey. In it will be everything that captures and inspires you: your purpose and passion, vision and goals, values and principles, mottos and affirmations—whatever you see as essential for a rich and fulfilling life. It's your personal manual for living.

On the road to freedom, it's powerful to have a guidebook of tips, tools, and insights. Start your own today and add to it as you go. Fill it with whatever you learn as you grow.

Who said you couldn't have a manual for living?

To understand the heart and mind of a person, look not at what he has already achieved, but at what he aspires to.
—Kahlil Gibran

DAY 117
CHANGE YOUR THOUGHTS AND CHANGE EVERYTHING

Many of us live in a state of chronic reaction, wondering what the heck we are going to feel at any given moment. We seem to think our circumstances determine our realities. We look at things as cause and effect.

But events don't simply cause emotions. And we are not victims of circumstance. It's the belief that gets activated within us that actually determines how we feel.

"See, nothing ever goes my way." "No one respects me." "I always get overlooked." "I can't trust anyone." Beliefs like these will continue negatively influencing what you feel and how you experience life.

Events don't make you feel what you feel. It's what you tell yourself about them that matters. Start paying attention to your thoughts and you just might reveal some harmful patterns. You might expose long-standing negative beliefs that are not serving you.

You get to choose how you feel. You choose how you experience life. It's all within your power.

A man sooner or later discovers that he is the
master-gardener of his soul, the director of his life.
—James Allen

DAY 118
BEGIN AGAIN

On the road to personal freedom, we have to accept some failure. In fact, we need to embrace it. It's instrumental to our growth.

Failure is an opportunity to learn something new. Failure means we tried, we put ourselves out there, we did something, and we have the chance to learn something about ourselves.

If you don't want to fail, you definitely don't have to. Just don't try. But know that if you don't try, you will never succeed.

Successful people fail. They use their failures to learn and grow. They allow themselves to begin again—and again. The only true failures are those who never try.

Which kind of person are you going to be?

One fails forward toward success.
—Charles F. Kettering

DAY 119
BE GRATEFUL

We have limited space in these brains of ours. As such, we need to carefully choose the thoughts with which we fill them. By choosing positive thoughts, we squeeze out the negative. In the same way, we get to choose the emotions with which we fill our hearts. In so doing, we choose what we squeeze out.

Maybe your heart has been filled with sadness. Perhaps you have been clinging to negativity for as long as you can remember. You can't imagine anything else.

You can change your internal experience. It all begins with a decision. If you want to do away with resentment—with the anger that comes from feeling like a victim—the decision is pretty clear. Choose gratitude. Let in light and you will eliminate the dark. It's inevitable.

Give it a try. Fill your heart with gratitude, and see what happens. Gratitude and resentment simply can't coexist.

The unthankful heart...discovers no mercies;
but let the thankful heart sweep through the day and,
as the magnet finds the iron, so it will find,
in every hour, some heavenly blessings!
—Henry Ward Beecher

DAY 120
ADVOCATE FOR YOUR OWN PURPLENESS

I once heard someone talk about advocating for her own "purpleness." I just loved the concept!

She was discussing her tendencies to self-deny, "play to the audience," and alter herself to suit others. She said it was as if she was one color, but everyone in her life wanted her to be another—and she willingly obliged.

If someone wanted her to be green, she was green. If someone expected her to be yellow, she was yellow. In reality, though, she was purple—she had been all along. She just hadn't let anyone know.

She said she had been working on standing up for herself, embracing and honoring who she was, and being unapologetic about it. Now she advocates for her own purpleness!

Are you a chameleon? Do you change your color to suit others? Perhaps it's time to stand up for who you are.

If you are ashamed to stand by your colors,
you had better seek another flag.
—Author unknown

DAY 121
FIND HOPE IN THE DARKEST OF DAYS

The darkness challenges and inspires. The darkness is where we hunt for our most important answers—and find them. Sure, the bright times enliven and excite, but it's the darkness that stimulates growth, tests our perspective, and reminds us of life's preciousness.

As I sat tearfully on the ground next to our thirteen-year-old lab on one of his final days, my daughter, Daisy, kneeled down next to me, put her hand reassuringly on my shoulder, and said, in all her six-year-old wisdom, "It's okay, Mom. Wompa needs a good dog up there in heaven." (Wompa is her deceased grandfather.) Ah yes, there always *is* another side to the coin, as my sweet little girl reminded me.

When things seem too difficult to bear—when we feel powerless in the face of circumstances outside our control—what can we do? We can look for the meaning. We can look for the lessons. We can look for the beauty.

The darkness challenges you to dig deep. If you accept the challenge, it's amazing what you will find.

> *I said to my soul, be still, and wait...*
> *So the darkness shall be the light,*
> *and the stillness the dancing.*
> —T. S. Eliot

DAY 122
TAKE THE AUTHENTIC ROUTE

When you find yourself questioning what to do, how to be, and what to say—when you are overwhelmed by all those *shoulds* and *ought tos* swirling around in your head and you can't quite figure out the right thing to do—get back to basics. Keep it simple. Be you.

Shape-shifting to suit others, altering who you are to keep those around you comfortable, betraying yourself just to please…these patterns are not only unhealthy; they're crazy-making.

We can't please everyone. Trying to do so only keeps us anxious, burdened, and distracted from who we truly are. It's an impossible goal.

Authenticity is the way out. Authenticity is the route to freedom from all of the chaos and confusion. When in doubt, be honest. Say what you think and feel. Ask for what you want and need.

When in doubt, be real.

One's real life is often the life that one does not lead.
—Oscar Wilde

DAY 123
SEIZE THE MOMENT

"I wonder if I will stick with it." "I hope I will follow through with my plan." "I pray I can do it." We say these things all the time. It's as if we have no say in how we show up. It's as if life happens to us and we simply wait and wonder what will be.

But life is not a waiting game. It isn't a passive experience. Life is about taking action. It's about making things happen. It's about setting goals—and achieving them. It's about shaping your own destiny.

The wait-and-see approach keeps you in a reactive position in your own life. It keeps you disempowered, helpless, and at the mercy of circumstance. Worse yet, a great deal of time and energy is expended waiting and wondering, trying to figure out what will be.

There are enough unknowns out there—unknowns over which we are indeed powerless. But in a world of uncertainty and unpredictability, there is one thing you can know for sure: that you will show up for yourself and take action on your own behalf.

Life is what you make it. So get proactive. Make the most of the moment. It might not come again.

We are always getting ready to live but never living.
—Ralph Waldo Emerson

DAY 124
QUIET THE BAND IN THE BASEMENT

Some call it the committee in our head. Some say it's the band in the basement. I see it as a board of directors sitting at a boardroom table, voting on every move we make, making decisions about things like our worth, value, and personal rights. And it's crazy-making.

Whatever we call it, it's that gang of voices within that relentlessly chimes in on every move we make, chattering about what we should do and how we should be, always with an undercurrent of criticism and judgment.

The committee. The band. The board of directors. It's time to dismiss them. It's time to be the sole decision maker in your own life, sit at the head of your own boardroom table, and decide for yourself who you are and how you are going to be.

It can change your life.

The greatest discovery of my generation is that human beings
can alter their lives by altering their attitude of mind.
—William James

DAY 125
PRESERVE YOUR SELF-IMAGE

Letting others determine our self-image is risky business.

Doing so means we can never count on what we are going to think and feel about ourselves, because it's all based on externals. Our sense of self fluctuates. Our self-image is high or low, positive or negative, all depending on what others seem to think of us. It doesn't have to be this way. We simply have it backwards.

Self-image is not the sum total of how you seem to the world. It isn't what others tell you about yourself. It isn't your persona or over-all package. Self-image is your opinion of *you*—and yours alone. It is based on who you are at your core and what you think and feel about who you are. It isn't up for debate by anyone else.

When you think about self-image, remember what it is. Remember that it's entirely within your control.

Knowledge of the self is the mother of all knowledge.
So it is incumbent on me to know my self, to know it completely,
to know its minutiae, its characteristics, its subtleties, and its very atoms.
—Khalil Gibran

DAY 126
MANAGE YOUR OWN REALITY

Ever heard, "You only think about yourself," or "It's all about you, isn't it?" You know what? It is.

While comments like these are clearly intended to be some kind of personal indictment, there is truth to them. Much of the time it is indeed about us.

If you're speaking up for what you want or need—if you're expressing your truth—it *is* about you. If you're setting a boundary—if you're advocating for yourself—it *is* about you. If you're letting someone know what does or doesn't work for you, it *is* about you. If you're taking care of yourself in some way, it's *also* about you—and it's okay for it to be.

This isn't to say don't think about others. I'm not recommending a me-myself-and-I kind of mindset. This is simply a reminder that yours is the only reality you can manage. And there is nothing wrong with self-advocacy, although it can definitely get a bad rap. There's nothing wrong with being strong, empowered, and self-directed. It's your right and responsibility to show up for yourself.

The next time someone says, "It's all about you, isn't it?" how about saying, "Why yes, this is about me. Who else would it be about?"

If you haven't the strength to impose your own terms upon life,
you must accept the terms it offers you.
—T. S. Eliot

DAY 127
LIVE A SUCCESSFUL LIFE

What makes for a successful life? Is it something internal or external? Is it about doing or being? Is it how we show up or who we are?

Each of us has to come to terms with what we believe about success. How we define it is of the utmost importance. It shapes what we feel about ourselves and the lives we live.

If we make success contingent on external circumstances, we'll find ourselves frequently disappointed. It's also a trap if we base it on good fortune. Making success dependent on us and us alone holds far greater promise. Even better is making it contingent on who we are, not what we do.

Stop wondering if you will ever be successful. Stop questioning if your life could be considered a successful one. If you show up authentically—if you make your life an expression of who you are—you're nothing short of a screaming success.

When you come to see a successful life as a life authentically lived, your path becomes clear—and success is entirely within your reach.

A successful life is one that is lived through understanding and pursuing one's own path, not chasing after the dreams of others.
—Chin Ning Chu

DAY 128
LET FEAR TEACH YOU

On the path to personal freedom, we need to honor and give voice to our fears. We need to take the risk of sounding weak—at least to our own self-critical ears. We need to cry. We need to scream. We need to feel.

Let fear instruct you. Allow it to motivate and inform you. As you watch yourself reacting fearfully to life, ask, "Where is this fear coming from? Is this who I choose to be? What can I learn here?"

In denying fear—in avoiding and running from it—we miss out on some potent lessons. We miss out on the power of choosing how we will face life's challenges. We miss out on the gifts of walking through our own darkness and maintaining our connection with self all the while.

Embrace your humanness, allow yourself to feel, and grow through fear.

Fear is the needle that pierces us that it
may carry a thread to bind us to heaven.
—James Hastings

DAY 129
HEAL THE CORE, HEAL YOUR LIFE

Does it feel like all you do is apply Band-Aids to whatever hurts and expect them to do the trick? The truth is, healing happens from within.

Whatever is going on at your core, find out what it is. Maybe it's a fundamental self-esteem issue, a damaged boundary system, or a distorted belief system. Perhaps it's the lingering trauma of unmet wants and needs, or the pain of neglect, abuse, or abandonment.

Identify it and face it. Otherwise, it will continue to own you. It will distort how you show up in this life.

Don't settle for quick fixes. Go deep and heal yourself from within. Heal your core and you can heal your life.

Every human being is the author of his own health or disease.
—Buddha

DAY 130
GET STARTED

Don't wait for the ideal conditions in order to show up in this life. Don't wait for stars to be in perfect alignment in order to take action. Stop waiting for permission. Come to your own assistance now.

We tend to postpone self-care, delay our dreams, and put ourselves on hold, waiting for the right time to do things for ourselves. On the road to personal freedom, this has to change.

Do whatever it takes, regardless of present conditions, to come to your own assistance. If the timing doesn't feel perfect, do it anyway. If it seems too difficult to make a change, make the change anyway.

No more waiting for things to be just right. The time is now.

You must take action now that will move you towards your goals.
Develop a sense of urgency in your life.
—Les Brown

DAY 131
DO IT BECAUSE IT'S WORTH THE RIDE

Do you do things simply for the joy of it all? If not, it's time.

Think of the juicy life you could be living if you took chances, embraced experience for experience sake, lived life for the thrill of it, and jumped in and fully engaged. Think about what you're missing when you don't.

Once in a while you have to take a risk, put yourself out there, and enjoy the ride.

The person who risks nothing, does nothing, has nothing, is nothing, and becomes nothing. He may avoid suffering and sorrow, but he simply cannot learn and feel and change and grow and love and live.
—Leo F. Buscaglia

DAY 132
CHANGE YOURSELF

We wait for people to change. We wait for circumstances and situations to change. We think we would feel better if things around us would just change!

When our circumstances change, we do feel better. The person we have been hurt by changes his or her tune. The financial stress we have been under is somehow relieved. The opportunity we have been waiting for comes knockin'. We get a reprieve from whatever discomfort we have been in. And we let out a sigh of relief.

But what happens when circumstances don't keep you comfortable? What happens when things don't change? That's when YOU need to change.

Create your own comfort. Be your own change agent. No more waiting around for things to align themselves to suit you. Make things happen for yourself. This is the empowered and liberated way.

Take ownership of your own reality. Remember, if things aren't going to change, then YOU need to change.

Things do not change; we change.
—Henry David Thoreau

DAY 133
BELIEVE IN YOUR DREAMS

You have dreams. You might not be aware of it, but you do. We all do. The challenge is bringing them to life.

Many of us have lost touch with the dreamer within. We have suppressed our yearnings and passions for so long that our light has become hidden. What's more, we talk ourselves out of dreaming and out of any prospect of achieving our dreams. We tell ourselves that dreaming is a frivolous luxury afforded only a few.

Do you feel passion within you? Do you have ideas and curiosities? Do you have hope and enthusiasm? Do certain things excite and activate you? If so, you are a dreamer. If not, you've likely talked yourself out of your dreams without even knowing it.

There's only one person who needs to believe in your dreams. There's only one person who needs to believe they are worthy no matter what anyone else thinks.

Get out of your way and believe in your dreams. If you don't, who will?

We all have our own life to pursue, our own kind of dream to be weaving.
And we all have some power to make wishes come true,
as long as we keep believing.
—Louisa May Alcott

DAY 134
THANK EVERYTHING

We can be so selective with our gratitude. We reserve it for happy endings, as if thankfulness is only appropriate when things work out as we want them to. We are grateful when things feel good.

But what do we do with pain and suffering? What do we do when things don't work out? Do we simply hold our breath, surviving life's difficulties, waiting for the next good thing for which to be thankful?

Being grateful part-time doesn't work. Being choosy about what deserves our thankfulness keeps us half-satisfied. Life will feel unstable. Our peace will be unpredictable.

Be grateful for it all. Embrace every life experience—the good and the bad, the joy and the pain—as a growth opportunity. You might wrestle with this concept at times, especially while in the valleys of life, but if you look for the gratitude, you will find it.

Try not to be so focused on happy endings that you lose the beauty along the way. Practice gratitude no matter what.

Don't cry because it ended. Smile because it happened.
—Dr. Seuss

DAY 135
AIM HIGH AND KEEP YOUR FEET ON THE GROUND

It is good to be grounded and rooted in reality. It's also important to dream and to look ahead to the future. The good news is you don't have to choose between the two.

Being overly grounded doesn't serve us. It stifles imagination and inspiration. It inhibits our life force and limits our joy. Over time, all our pragmatism can turn into pessimism. We lack enjoyment and freedom in life.

Having our heads entirely in the stars, however, doesn't work either. Our lack of practicality can fuel disappointment and discouragement. We find ourselves struggling with the day-to-day. We tend to fall short of the mark in our own eyes.

Having lived in each extreme, I find the key is balance between the two. Create your vision, let yourself dream, and aspire to something. At the same time, keep your feet in today. That way, you can make your dreams a reality one step at a time.

Realism and vision are not mutually exclusive. The sweet spot is somewhere in the middle.

Realistic people with practical aims are rarely as realistic or practical in the long run of life as the dreamers who pursue their dreams.
—Hans Selye

DAY 136
TAKE THE FUN OUT OF DYSFUNCTION

It seems we have fooled ourselves into thinking it's somehow fun to be dysfunctional—that chaos is a good thing.

Dysfunction is bondage. Whether it's our own unhealthy living, a problematic relationship we are in, or perhaps a toxic family system, dysfunction locks us into reactive, well-patterned grooves—mentally, emotionally, and relationally.

The patterns might be familiar, but they're not healthy. And we don't have to accept them. We certainly don't need to make light of them. Just because things have become functionally dysfunctional, so to speak, doesn't mean they're okay.

Confront the dysfunction. Make a decision to liberate yourself from it. It won't take long to see that the very thing you've been tolerating has been dragging you down.

There isn't any fun in dysfunction. Find your fun somewhere else.

If you do not change direction, you may end up where you are heading.
—Lao Tzu

DAY 137
SET YOURSELF UP TO SUCCEED

Often, by biting off more than we can chew, we set ourselves up to fail.

We create daunting goals, expect too much too soon, and hold ourselves to impossible standards, not thinking to break our intentions down into manageable and achievable pieces. We end up flip-flopping between hopeful and dejected, between riding high and feeling low, and between visionary and underachiever.

Set yourself up for success instead. Decide to build faith in yourself one step at a time. Grow your self-confidence by doing the things that will actually build confidence. Set achievable goals, and feel good about reaching them.

No more generating disappointment for yourself. Take things in bite-sized pieces. Move gradually and thoughtfully along your journey to personal freedom, creating the best possible scenarios for turning your dreams into reality.

The ability to convert ideas to things is the secret to outward success.
—Henry Ward Beecher

DAY 138
FIND THE SWEET IN THE BITTERSWEET

In the toughest of times there exists beauty. In the depths of grief, in the heart of turmoil, there is something beautiful to be discovered. If you haven't found it yet, keep looking.

In the midst of each of my parent's passing, as I kept vigil at their bedsides, I saw them actively slipping away from this life—and there was something beautiful in it.

It was bittersweet in every sense of the word, as are our most trying life experiences. The bitter was obvious and extraordinarily painful, as I faced the reality of loss. But there was sweet as well. There is always the sweet.

It was a privilege to be there for them from the beginning of their decline to those final moments. It was an honor to give back to those who had given so much. It was the most tender, honest, and vulnerable kind of shared experience—the deepest of human connection. It was rich, poignant, and powerful.

Remember the sweet in the bittersweet. It might be hard to find, but if you look for it, you will find it. When you do, you will find comfort, strength, and healing. When you do, you will find the spiritual side of whatever it is you are going through.

To live is to suffer, to survive is to find some meaning in the suffering.
—Friedrich Nietzsche

DAY 139
RECALIBRATE

Many of us unknowingly limit our own pleasure and excitement. We do so because our emotional set point is too low. It's time to recalibrate.

Just as our bodies have certain weight set points, we also have emotional set points—baselines to which we consistently revert. Does your emotional set point need resetting?

Perhaps it feels like you can't get anywhere. You have growth spurts here and there—periods of motivation and empowerment—but time and time again you revert back to self-limitation and stagnation. There's likely some negativity within that needs to be rooted out.

Notice what happens when you let yourself dream a little, when you think about what you want out of life, and when you engage that visionary part of you. What thoughts immediately follow? Are they encouraging or discouraging?

It's the discouraging self-talk that keeps your set point where it is. It's the negativity that brings you back to that baseline time and time again.

Make a decision to break free from self-limiting thinking. Create new emotional goals. Set the bar higher. Reset your emotional set point and allow yourself the joy you deserve.

All our dreams can come true—if we have the courage to pursue them.
—Walt Disney

DAY 140
PRIME THE PUMP

The stimuli we expose ourselves to are often called primes. They prime the pump, so to speak, prompting us to think, feel, and behave in certain ways. Incorporate positive primes into your every day and you can profoundly influence your overall outlook.

Prime yourself with quotes, sayings, and affirmations. Surround yourself with things you love, with positive memories, and with visual mementos. Create a vision board or dream board. Keep something symbolic with you like a stone or a coin to remind you of the journey you are on, to keep an intention front and center, or to remind you of your inner child and the importance of self-care.

Pay attention to what inspires, nurtures, and motivates you. Notice what helps you feel good about yourself and your life. See what makes you feel warm inside. Then weave those reminders into your daily living. It will shift the way you experience your world.

We all need reminding, so prime yourself. Your life will bear the fruits.

The positive thinker sees the invisible,
feels the intangible, and achieves the impossible.
—Author unknown

DAY 141
MEET YOURSELF WHERE YOU ARE

We bring such suffering upon ourselves when we resist where we are and what we are experiencing, when we tell ourselves we shouldn't feel what we feel, and when we believe we should be somewhere we are not. We disallow our own realities, and in so doing, prolong distress, deepen pain, heighten anxiety, and make worse whatever it is we are experiencing.

It's never wise to deny or debate your own reality. Meet yourself right where you are instead. Accept what you are feeling, free from criticism and judgment.

Don't measure yourself and what you're feeling against some external standard that only makes you feel worse about where you are. Don't compare yourself to others. Have compassion for yourself. When necessary, take your own hand and gently nudge yourself forward. Do what a loving parent would do. Accept. Nurture. Encourage.

You need not complicate things by refusing to accept what you feel. It's so much simpler to meet yourself right where you are and to love yourself in that place.

I'm not afraid of storms, for I'm learning to sail my ship.
—Louisa May Alcott

DAY 142
LIVE AN EMOTIONALLY HONEST LIFE

The only thing worse than feeling uncomfortable feeings is blaming and shaming ourselves for having them, denying what we feel because what we feel isn't okay. Yet many of us do just this, and we suffer for it, both personally and relationally.

While we are more likely to skirt uncomfortable feelings, emotional dishonesty isn't limited to these. We often deny our more comfortable emotions as well. Basically, we play small emotionally. We tone ourselves down, deny what we feel, and dishonor who we are.

Emotional dishonesty blocks authenticity, inhibits personal freedom, and impedes healthy relations. Emotional honesty, on the other hand, is virtually synonymous with freedom. It releases us to feel what we feel and be who we are.

Liberate your emotions. If you're scared, seek comfort. If you're angry, work through it. If you feel guilty, make amends. If you feel shame, learn from it and release it. If you're hurting, reach out. If you have passion, engage it. If you feel love, express it. And if you feel joy, by all means, let it out.

What is uttered from the heart alone,
will win the hearts of others to your own.
—Johann Wolfgang von Goethe

DAY 143
LET GO

It tugs at the heart, boggles the mind, and puts the spirit to the test. It's called forgiveness. But what exactly is it?

Forgiveness, according to Merriam-Webster, is "to give up resentment." Many of us resist this relinquishing. We hide behind the security of our resentments and unforgiving spirits. We think they give us power. We think they give us control.

But as good as the payoffs of not forgiving may seem, the perks of forgiveness are better. Forgiveness opens the door to healing. It frees us from the past and from our painful attachments to it. Resentment drains our life force. Forgiveness replenishes it.

We all want the freedom of letting go—the freedom of forgiveness. But we need to be willing to do the footwork. No more holding on, clinging to resentments, clutching the illusion of power, and waiting for the kind of liberation that only comes with forgiveness.

The time is now. Let go.

There is a mental treatment guaranteed to cure every ill that flesh is heir to: Sit for half an hour every night and forgive everyone against whom you have any ill will or antipathy.
—Charles Filmore

DAY 144
HOLD OUT FOR JUICY LOVE

Watch out for being wishy-washy about the things you love, downplaying and diminishing your capacity for passion and enjoyment. Don't settle for a so-so existence. Don't resign yourself to *just okay*. Go for juicy love.

Notice what wakes you up and gets you going. Observe what feels exciting and irresistible to you. Pay attention to what ignites passion and hunger within. Where are you at the time? What are you doing? Who are you with? The objects of your affection say everything about who you are. They give your life direction and purpose.

Love takes many forms and has many outlets. So don't box yourself in with restrictions and conventions. There are no universal rules about love, about what you should or shouldn't love, or about how to go about doing it.

Love what you love. Don't question it; just love it. We all deserve juicy, sink-your-teeth-into-it kind of love in our lives.

We are all born for love. It is the principle of existence, and its only end.
—Benjamin Disraeli

DAY 145
GET TO KNOW YOURSELF

Each of us should know what we are good at. We should have a handle on our strengths and talents, our skills and natural capacities.

If you don't, it's time to get familiarized with yourself.

Take some personality and interest tests, read some insightful, thought-provoking books, and talk to those close to you about what they believe to be your gifts. Go on a quest to get to know yourself, and get excited about everything you find.

You need to know who you are in order to reach your potential. When you can soar with your strengths, whatever they are, you'll always be a success.

No one remains quite what he was when he recognizes himself.
—Thomas Mann

DAY 146
FIND YOUR ANSWERS WITHIN

We look for it everywhere. We look for it in our accomplishments, in status, in power, in our profession, in how we look, in our relationships, and in other people. What we are looking for is our missing piece.

We are looking for the part of us we think we were born without. We have convinced ourselves it's out there somewhere. But it's all an illusion. There is nothing out there that will give us what we are looking for. There is nothing outside of us that will complete us.

If you've been looking for your missing piece, you can stop looking. You are complete in and of yourself. All the answers to whatever you think you are lacking are within you—they always have been.

Think about how hard you've been looking for that missing piece. What if you knew you could stop trying? What if you knew you had been whole all along?

One's own self is well hidden from one's own self;
of all mines of treasure, one's own is the last to be dug up.
—Friedrich Nietzsche

DAY 147
DO IT NO MATTER WHAT

Living in a spirit of "no matter what" is about living from your core. It's a personal commitment. It's a promise to self. It's about consistency. It's about faith.

If you tend to be externally driven rather than internally directed, this concept is for you. If you tend to be swayed by the tides of other people's wants, needs, expectations, and judgments, if you let others tell you who you are, it's time to weave "no matter what" into your mindset.

Notice the power in these three little words. Feel the stability, strength, and permanence they bring. I am worthy and valuable *no matter what*. I love and honor myself *no matter what*. I forgive myself *no matter what*. I honor my truth *no matter what*. I will be okay *no matter what!*

Adopt a *no matter what* mindset, and live from that place. Give yourself the gift of a greater sense of permanence within. Give yourself the gift of "no matter what."

What lies behind us and what lies before us are
tiny matters compared to what lies within us.
—Ralph Waldo Emerson

DAY 148
PICK YOUR HEAD UP

Are you living life on autopilot?

Many of us who grew up in unhealthy early life circumstances were compelled to adapt along the way. Whether consciously or subconsciously, we learned to conform to the dysfunction around us by coping and tolerating. We learned to hold our breath and power through.

This survival mode often becomes a way of life. When it does, it backfires on us. The coping skills that at one time helped us get by end up robbing us of our ability to thrive later on. If we don't look them in the eye and deliberately outgrow them, our survival mechanisms become our bondage. The head down, grin-and-bear-it approach is no way to live.

But this is your present, not your past. You are an adult. You no longer need to simply endure. You are safe now. You can exhale and step into your life.

No more living life with your head down. Pick your head up and look straight ahead.

Life isn't about waiting for the storm to pass.
It's about learning to dance in the rain.
—Author unknown

DAY 149
CLEAN UP THAT BELIEF SYSTEM

The beliefs we hold about ourselves find their origins in life experience. If we were raised in nurturing, encouraging, and validating environments, characterized by healthy relationships, we likely came to believe in our worth and value. Through positive modeling and reinforcement, we developed a healthy and supportive belief system.

If we were raised in unhealthy environments, we came to believe something different. Seeds of insecurity got planted within us, and they find their way into our adult relationships. We choose partnerships in which we feel about ourselves the way we have felt before. We co-create dynamics reminiscent of our histories. We allow ourselves to be dishonored. We dishonor ourselves. We learned what we lived.

Thankfully, the story doesn't end here. If this sounds familiar to you, you are by no means out of luck. You just have some cleaning up to do.

I can believe anything, provided that it is quite incredible.
—Oscar Wilde

DAY 150
WASH YOUR BRAIN

Many of us got brainwashed early on, indoctrinated into a belief system that hasn't served us very well. Now it's time for a different kind of brainwashing.

It's time to out your belief system. It's time to reveal all the negative thinking contaminating it and design some new thoughts. It's time for a cleansing of that brain.

Uncover your core beliefs. See what's true for you and what isn't. See what's authentic and what never was. Create some healthy reframes for each thought which, over time, has become self-limiting. Then work these positive reframes until they become new beliefs. This is the essence of positive affirmation.

Whatever you do, don't live life on autopilot. Shake things up. Make a change.

It's time for a new kind of brainwashing.

All truly wise thoughts have been thoughts already thousands of times;
but to make them truly ours, we must think them over again honestly,
till they take root in our personal experience.
—Johann Wolfgang Von Goethe

DAY 151
COMMUNICATE BOUNDARIES

Personal boundaries are limits that protect and preserve our internal realities. They are an essential life skill. We can't maintain a sense of self without them.

But boundaries are more than invisible limits and borders. Boundaries actually speak. We express them in our communication with others, in how we share and how we listen. We teach people how to treat us by communicating healthy personal limits.

Boundaries express who we are. They define and preserve our truth. They allow us to speak from the first person, sharing freely our thoughts, feelings, wants, and needs. They enable us to listen respectfully as others do the same.

Boundaries also foster interdependence. They help us strike balance between autonomy and intimacy, between freedom and connection. We express who we are, and we celebrate who others are. We advocate for our wants and needs, and we give others permission to do so as well.

Cultivate healthy connections. Communicate your boundaries.

Boundaries are to protect life, not to limit pleasures.
—Edwin Louis Cole

DAY 152
TAKE YOUR BOUNDARIES WITH YOU

Boundaries are nothing short of self-preservation. They safeguard our identities. They enable us to feel secure, self-defined, grounded, and autonomous. They keep us from living in reaction. They enable us to show up and be who we are, no matter what.

If you struggle to maintain yourself out there in the world, then take a look at the state of your personal boundaries. If you frequently feel overwhelmed, anxious, and insecure, if it seems others rob you of your inner security, it's time to make a change.

Personal limit-setting doesn't always come naturally. For many of us, it's anything but natural. We have to be deliberate about working our boundaries. We have to be mindful about staying rooted in who we are, about protecting and preserving self.

Identify, respect, and maintain your personal boundaries. And by all means, never leave home without them!

Your personal boundaries protect the inner core
of your identity and your right to choices.
—Gerard Manley Hopkins

DAY 153
SHAPE YOUR REALITY

We often let other people's realities determine our own. If someone is sad, we feel sad. If someone is mad, we get mad. If someone does something immoral or unkind, it fires us up and robs us of our peace. If someone treats us poorly, we feel badly about ourselves for the rest of the day.

This is an unpredictable way to live. If we don't know what or how to feel until circumstance tells us, we never get to decide what kind of day we are going to have. We wait to see what happens before we know what to feel.

You can turn this around. It begins with a decision to take back the power over your own experiences.

Your reality is not the measure of what others think, feel, say or do, so stop letting others tell you what kind of day you're going to have. Don't let who they are determine who you are. Stop allowing them to occupy space in your brain, rent-free!

You and only you get to decide how you feel today.

In the long run, we shape our lives, and we shape ourselves.
The process never ends until we die. And the choices
we make are ultimately our own responsibility.
—Eleanor Roosevelt

DAY 154
BE JOYFUL

Do you live life in a state of negative anticipation? Is it robbing you of joy?

Living in pessimistic expectation steals our present. It contaminates the *now* with fear and worry. In trying to predict and prepare for the next unpleasant experience, we keep ourselves in a state of reaction. We invite into today what we fear about tomorrow. We are already reacting to our worst fears—and they haven't even happened yet.

Let go of that negative anticipation. Choose a positive attitude, and greet the future and whatever it brings with openness and hope. Have faith that whatever happens, you will meet the experience with the right attitude.

If you're going to plan for anything, plan for joy.

We plan our joys and sorrows long before we experience them.
—Kahlil Gibran

DAY 155
CLAIM YOUR RIGHT SIZE

Many of us shape-shift because we don't know how to be who we are. Sometimes we play small. Sometimes we play big. We have yet to claim our right size.

Maybe you've been keeping yourself a secret, hiding your light, dumbing yourself down because you don't think you deserve to stand in your power and be who you are. Perhaps you've been living large, playing to the audience, trying to be someone you're not because you think you have something to prove.

Either way, you've been a distortion of your authentic self.

It's time to stop misrepresenting yourself. No more playing small. No more trying to be big. Stop betraying who you are by changing your shape.

Claim your right size.

Always be a first-rate version of yourself,
instead of a second-rate version of somebody else.
—Judy Garland

DAY 156
LIVE FEARLESSLY

Take a close look at fear. Really examine it. See what's generating it. What thoughts have been driving your fear?

Are they thoughts of a wounded, vulnerable, and emotionally young you? Are they thoughts others handed to you along the way, which you ultimately adopted and internalized? What if you rewrote the script by which you've been living?

Fear is a natural emotion. We all have it. But it's the fear that's born out of a disempowered belief system that doesn't serve you. It's the fear that's generated by lies that stops you in your tracks. It's the fear of being who you truly are that holds you back. It's the fear of being fearless from which you need to break free.

Examine your thinking. Change the beliefs that need to be changed. Lighten the burden of fear.

Life is a process of becoming, a combination of states we have
to go through. Where people fail is that they wish to elect
a state and remain in it. This is a kind of death.
—Anais Nin

DAY 157
LET GO OF GUARANTEES

Do you wait for assurances before taking chances and making changes? Do you hold out for guarantees before taking a risk? Are you so attached to outcomes that you end up staying stuck?

I've always been fond of guarantees myself. I also know this propensity was stunting my growth. I was barking up the wrong trees for these guarantees, looking outside rather than within. Redirecting my attention has been life-changing.

Let go of the need for guarantees—at least the ones you can't control. Hold on to the one guarantee you can rightfully have—that you will show up fully and faithfully in your life today...and that one today at a time, you will continue doing so.

Life doesn't give us guarantees about what's coming down the pike. We can't script all outcomes. There's much that's outside our control. Let go of the need to know. Meet life boldly and fearlessly, right here, right now.

We must be willing to let go of the life we have planned,
so as to accept the life that is waiting for us.
—Joseph Campbel

DAY 158
IDENTIFY THE ME AND NOT ME

Each of us has an authentic self. It is how we came into this world. It is our core, our foundation, and our most enduring being.

Many of us also have an adapted self. This is our persona, our constructed personality, and our means of coping. It's how we learned to get by in this world. We may think the authentic and adapted selves are one and the same, but they are not.

We are not our adaptations, and our adaptations are not who we are. Maybe we have lived in survival mode so long it has become our normal, but normal isn't necessarily authentic.

Personal freedom hinges on our ability to disentangle the authentic from the adapted. We have to wake up to the fact that how we have been living our lives isn't necessarily a reflection of who we are.

As you awaken to the persona you've constructed, you will start learning about yourself. You will hear a voice within you saying, "Wait a second; that isn't who I am," and "That isn't who I know myself to be." You will find the person you have lost along the way.

You are not your adaptations. You are not who your history said you were. You are not always the measure of how you've been showing up.

The authentic you is waiting to be revealed.

If you don't get lost, there's a chance you may never be found.
—Author unknown

DAY 159
GIVE IT BACK
(IT WAS NEVER YOURS TO CARRY)

Shame is a natural human emotion. We all have it. It can also be toxic. It can become a condition. That shame might not even be our own.

When shame is something we carry for others, when it weighs us down and depletes our life force, when it's burdensome and self-defeating, something isn't right.

If you have been carrying around shame that isn't your own, the kind of shame that's attached to negative life experiences, to the ways others have treated you, it's time to give it back.

You were never meant to have it to begin with.

Getting over a painful experience is much like crossing monkey bars.
You have to let go at some point in order to move forward.
—Author unknown

DAY 160
FINISH UNFINISHED BUSINESS

Ever wonder why your spirit doesn't feel entirely free? Why you feel burdened and held back? You likely have unfinished business.

It might be a lingering resentment. An old hurt. A truth you never spoke. A right you never claimed. Whatever it is, it could be draining you, keeping you from stepping into the now.

It's time to speak up. It's time to forgive. It's time to learn from your history and let go.

Freedom is found in finishing that unfinished business.

Forgiveness is the fragrance that the
violet sheds on the heel that has crushed it.
—Mark Twain

DAY 161
DO IT WITH GUSTO

"Gusto" is a great word that means "vigorous enjoyment" and "zest." Are you living with vigorous enjoyment? Are you living with zest?

Make note of where the oomph is lacking. Now imagine what it would be like to pour your heart into life—to infuse it with gusto. Make a decision to crank up the volume on your life.

Pursue your passions with gusto. Speak your truth with gusto. Feel your feelings with gusto. Love and laugh with gusto.

Live life to the fullest. And do it with gusto!

To do anything truly worth doing, I must not stand back shivering and thinking of the cold and danger, but jump in with gusto and scramble through as well as I can.
—Og Mandino

DAY 162
KEEP IT UP

When something works for us—I mean, *really works*—what do we often do? We STOP.

Counterintuitive as it is, we resist the things we know to be beneficial. Perhaps it's fear. Perhaps it's a feeling of unworthiness. Perhaps we are so convinced we will never feel good that we discontinue the things that feel good before we have to be disappointed.

Whatever the reason, we do things backwards. We stop doing what works and we continue doing what doesn't.

If you resemble this pattern, it's time to address it. Why do you resist self-care? Why do you fight what's working? Why the easy self-abandonment?

Turn this around. Do the things that work for you, and do them long enough that they become part of you. Keep those healthy intentions front and center, revisiting them regularly. Honor your commitments to yourself.

From here on, try something different. If it's working, keep it up!

Success is not final, failure is not fatal:
it is the courage to continue that counts.
—Winston Churchill

DAY 163
CREATE A NOT-TO-DO LIST

Many of us are addicted to our to-do lists. We feel anxious without them. We come up with endless tasks we think we have to do—and have to do now. But what do we do when those lists become burdensome? What do we do when a to-do mentality gets the best of us?

We can create a not-to-do list.

Perhaps you'll decide not to overwork and over-busy yourself. Maybe you'll choose not to deny yourself relaxation and downtime. You might decide not to do for others at the expense of yourself. You might commit to stop shaming and blaming yourself. Maybe you'll decide not to drive yourself to do every item on your to-do list!

To-do lists are oppressive. Not-to-do lists are liberating. Think about what you can eliminate today and how you might lighten the load. Get excited about it.

The time to relax is when you don't have time for it.
—Sydney J. Harris

DAY 164
BELIEVE THE GOOD THINGS ABOUT YOURSELF

Is it easier to buy into the negative messages about yourself than the positive ones? Do you readily accept the not-so-good because it's a fit for what you already believe as true?

If so, you clearly got lied to along the way. Whether directly or indirectly, overtly or covertly, you have been fed negative messages about who you are—messages that, over time, have shaped a painful internal belief system. You adopted them as true.

The good news is you can turn this around. You can come to believe the truths about who you are. Just be prepared for it to take some time.

You didn't come to believe the lies overnight, and it will take time to believe the truths. Just be patient. And even if it feels false to affirm yourself, which it most likely will, don't give up. You wouldn't stop speaking loving truths to a child just because he or she wasn't buying them, would you?

Devote yourself to the task of loving yourself. Get motivated. Take action. Only then will you begin to believe the good things.

It ain't what they call you, it's what you answer to.
—W. C. Fields

DAY 165
CHIP AWAY THE EXCESS

When asked how he created his statue of *David*, Michelangelo is reported to have said, "The masterpiece was in there all the time. I just chipped away the excess."

What if you adopted the same perspective regarding your own inner beauty? What if, instead of searching for yourself out there somewhere, you looked within? What if, instead of adding layers to yourself in a hunt for identity, you made it your goal to reveal yourself?

Pay attention to the excesses in your life—to the things that keep the masterpiece that is you hidden. Get ready to shed some layers.

Your true self lies within. Your uniqueness and splendor may not be visible, but they are there, just waiting to be discovered.

Start chipping away the excess.

You were born an original. Don't die a copy.
—John Mason

DAY 166
WELCOME NEWNESS

Just because we have one way of doing things doesn't mean it's the only way. Just because we have well-worn grooves of patterned thinking and behavior doesn't mean we aren't meant to challenge them. There's nothing progressive about *same old, same old*.

A progressive life is a life of newness. Newness is the source of learning, growth, and personal evolution.

Welcome the new into your life and into your every day. Shake things up. Get excited about doing so.

See how awake and alive you feel.

Sometimes we are lucky enough to know that our lives have been changed, to discard the old, embrace the new, and run headlong down an immutable course.
—Jacques-Yves Cousteau

DAY 167
PROTECT THE NOW

Are you so preoccupied with what happened *then* and what could happen *when* that you're not present now? Are the past and future robbing you of today?

Pain, regret, and rumination: these are the past creeping into today. Fear, anxiety, and anticipation: these are the future infringing upon it. Some of us live in yesterday, some of us in tomorrow, and some of us have one foot in each. Either way, we are unplugging from our present.

If you have unresolved hurts, heal them. If you have fear about the future, manage it. Whatever you do, don't let past pain or fear about the future dictate how you experience today. If you do, you will be limiting yourself. You will end up feeling powerless and helpless.

You can't buy back your past. And without a crystal ball, you can't accurately predict tomorrow. Rewriting yesterday and trying to forecast tomorrow are unrealistic goals. You don't have that power.

Protect and preserve the *now* instead. Focus on what's right in front of you. Put your energy where your power is.

Yesterday is history. Tomorrow is a mystery.
Today is a gift. That's why we call it "the present."
—Eleanor Roosevelt

DAY 168
ALLOW YOURSELF TO FEEL

Many of us deny our emotions. We stuff and suppress them, avoiding anything and everything emotionally uncomfortable. We lie to ourselves, thinking it's good to zip up, that it's noble to be stoic. We deny our humanness.

The truth is, if we want to live liberated lives, we need to liberate our emotions. We need to experience and express the fullness of who we are. We need to get real in order to get well.

Don't be alarmed by emotional discomfort. Vulnerability isn't a setback. It's simply your humanness.

Allowing your feelings is a beautiful thing.

The great art of life is sensation, to feel that we exist, even in pain.
—Lord Byron

DAY 169
TAKE YOURSELF OUT OF THE EQUATION

It's dangerous to over-personalize. It's dangerous to tell ourselves that every pain we experience is about us.

It's the wounded, young part of us who tends to do this—who thinks other people's behavior is somehow the measure of our own worth and value. The insecurity within says that if someone treats us poorly, we must have deserved it. If something hurts us, it must be about us.

People will be unkind sometimes. Life will be unkind. It doesn't mean it's a reflection of who you are and what you do or don't deserve. Making it such only keeps you in a reactive, emotionally charged posture in life.

Detach from other people's behavior. Stop looking for reasons to feel responsible for their actions. Stop blaming yourself for your pain. There is great freedom in this detachment. There is freedom in taking yourself out of every equation.

Just because it hurts you doesn't mean it's about you.

Always behave like a duck—keep calm and unruffled
on the surface, but paddle like the devil underneath.
—Jacob Braudealwya

DAY 170
SLOW IT DOWN

When our thoughts are racing, we need to slow them down. We need to take a breath and examine our thinking. Only then can we make needed adjustments in what we are telling ourselves.

When we relax, we can see things clearly. We are able to identify intrusive thoughts and find the static in our thinking. We get into observer mode with ourselves.

The next time you are feeling anxious and overwhelmed, give yourself a timeout. As the mind gets tranquil, answers will appear.

Slow down and enjoy life. It's not only the scenery you miss by going too fast—you also miss the sense of where you are going and why.
—Eddie Cantor

DAY 171
RECOVER YOUR WHOLENESS

Do you feel imcomplete? Half whole? As if you're always looking for that missing piece? You have a hunger for wholeness.

This hunger keeps you searching for the rest of you—for the part you disowned along the way. Maybe your history didn't let you be who you were. Maybe you didn't feel safe, accepted, or nurtured. Knowingly or unknowingly, you rejected aspects of yourself. Perhaps you felt you had to.

But we are not supposed to divorce our humanness or deny who we are. This just isn't the natural order of things.

We are meant for wholeness. We are meant to lean into who we are, accept what makes us unique, grow with our strengths, learn from our weaknesses, and embrace the whole package.

Identify the missing piece for which you have been longing. Commit yourself to owning again what you have disowned. Open yourself to wholeness.

When you come together with that missing piece, you will experience a sense of selfhood like never before.

Remember, you were built for wholeness.

You are all things. Denying, rejecting, judging, or hiding from any aspect of your total being creates pain and results in a lack of wholeness.
—Joy Page

DAY 172
PUMP UP THE GOOD VOLUME

You can magnify the good or the not-so-good. You get to decide.

Through what kind of lens are you looking at life? Has history distorted your perspective? Is your attitude more about your past than your present?

It's time to clear the lens and embrace what's right in front of you. No more letting what *was* determine how you experience what *is*. Update that outdated attitude.

Today, you decide what you magnify. Today, you choose your perspective. No one else gets to choose it for you.

Crank up the volume on the positive. Update that outdated attitude.

Your living is determined not so much by what life brings to you as by the attitude you bring to life; not so much by what happens to you as by the way your mind looks at what happens.
—Kahlil Gibran

DAY 173
MOVE INTO I CAN

Years ago I embarked on an "I can" experiment. That's when things really began shifting.

"I can" motivates. "I can" inspires. "I can" gives us a sense of direction and propels us into tomorrow. "I can" brings us closer to who we are.

Picture yourself living in a spirit of "I can." Imagine the power of seeing possibility where you once saw limitation, strength where you once saw weakness, and doors open where they once seemed closed.

What would it be like to believe in your dreams? To have faith in your potential? To let yourself shine?

Create some "I can" statements. Say them to yourself regularly. Inspire your way to a wonderful life.

Whether you think you can, or you think you can't—you're right.
—Henry Ford

DAY 174
LIVE IN A SPIRIT OF THANKFULNESS

We have these prescribed times when we say grace. We have set occasions for expressing gratitude. Mealtimes, holidays, and other special celebrations are when we make a point of being grateful. But grace isn't just for mealtime.

Why put boundaries around gratitude? Why relegate thankfulness to special occasions? If you're looking to cultivate a happy heart, this needs to change.

Take grace out of the box and spread it around. Let it spring from your soul anytime and anywhere. Let it find its way into everything you do, into all you experience.

Live in a spirit of thankfulness. Part-time gratitude won't do.

Saying thank you is more than good manners. It is good spirituality.
—Alfred Painter

DAY 175
LET GO OF RESENTMENT

It has been said that resentment is like taking poison and waiting for the other person to die.

We think resentment gives us power. Like a trump card we keep in our back pocket, we hold on to it, thinking it serves us somehow. We pull it out when we need a shot of control or one-upmanship, or when we want to flex a little muscle. We don't want to let it go.

But resentment only hurts us. It drains our life force. It keeps us depressed, disappointed, and bitter. It isn't power at all, only the illusion of it.

Resentment is victim anger—the kind of anger that comes from a victim position. Crack our exterior and we feel anything but powerful. We actually feel weak and wounded inside.

Let go of that victim anger. It gets you nowhere. Look at why you feel victimized, and take responsibility for your own healing. Parent those hurts with love and tenderness, rather than staying in that emotional holding pattern of resentment.

Your power lies in letting go, not in holding on.

Anger will never disappear so long as thoughts of resentment are cherished in the mind. Anger will disappear just as soon as thoughts of resentment are forgotten.
—Buddha

DAY 176
IDENTIFY THE REAL YOU

For many of us, there exists an inner battle. We doubt, debate, and resist ourselves. Sometimes we can't even stand ourselves. We flip-flop between acceptance and judgment, between peace and angst, between love and disdain for ourselves. We wonder why. Which voice within us is real?

Inside of each of us there exists our core. It's the truth of who we are—the way we came into this world. It's our enduring self. We might also have a persona on board, a constructed self who confuses matters and causes us to question who we truly are.

This persona is a composite of messages we have internalized, rules we have tried to live by, and coping mechanisms we have adopted along the way. It's the self we created to get by in this world. It's not a true self. It's a fabrication.

The battle inside you might be the conflict between authentic and inauthentic, between internal and external, or between truth and fiction. You have the power to quiet this inner struggle. You have the power to shed what is false and lean into who you are.

You have the power to get real.

And remember, no matter where you go, there you are.
—Confucius

DAY 177
GIVE YOUR AFFIRMATIONS LIFE

Positive affirmations are more than warm, fuzzy thoughts. Positive affirmations change lives. They program the mind the way commands program a computer, and in so doing, they change habits, behaviors, attitudes…even the shape of an existence.

Turn your self-defeating mindset on its heels. Banish negative thoughts by replacing them with positive ones. Take one harmful thought at a time, reframe it into its exact opposite, and repeat the new thought with conviction and desire. By transforming your thinking, you can transform everything.

Positive affirmations are not magic. They don't work on their own. We have to work them. Over time, however, we come to believe them. Over time, they become a way of life.

Breathe into your affirmations. Imagine them in action. Don't just leave them on a page. Live them.

The ancestor of every action is a thought.
—Ralph Waldo Emerson

DAY 178
FOCUS ON LIVING IN ALIGNMENT

Fear not; you don't have to get there, wherever *there* might be. Happiness is not a destination. Happiness is walking in line with your true nature.

In other words, you don't necessarily have to publish that book; you only need to write. You don't have to become that accomplished musician; you only have to play your music. You don't have to achieve your ultimate goal—not right now and not necessarily how you envision it. You need only live in alignment with who you are and what you love.

Step into your passion. Enjoy what you love, and go after your dreams. And remember, the power is in the pursuit.

A life of meaning is a life lived in alignment. That's where true satisfaction is found.

The life of inner peace, being harmonious and
without stress, is the easiest type of existence.
—Norman Vincent Peale

DAY 179
BE SPIRITUAL, PRACTICE BOUNDARIES

Boundaries often get a bad rap. They can be seen as walls, as lines in the sand others are not permitted to cross, and as impenetrable barriers that divide rather than unite. Personal boundaries conjure up some negative associations.

But healthy personal boundaries are anything but divisive. Healthy boundaries are about honor and respect. They foster interdependence. They are courteous, relational, and responsible.

Personal boundaries are a system of limit-setting that allows us to respectfully acknowledge where we end and others begin. They are the invisible borders that protect and preserve our own realities. They enable us to hold our own space, honor who we are, and allow others to be who they are.

Some boundary mantras are: "I respect myself, and I respect you too," "I honor my reality, and I honor yours as well," and "I stand in my truth, and I give you that same right."

Boundaries facilitate healthy interactions. They cultivate esteem and understanding. They truly are a spiritual practice.

Good fences make good neighbors.
—Robert Frost

DAY 180
PRESERVE THYSELF

If you see it you can be it.

It's a classic visualization premise, and it applies well to the concept of personal boundaries. If we can see our boundaries, we can live within them. If we can visualize the personal limits that protect and contain us, we can more effectively maintain them.

Conjure up some imagery to capture the essence of your boundaries. A bubble, a bell jar, a fence…whatever your image, its purpose is to keep harmful things out and welcome helpful things in. Boundaries are essential for managing our realities and preserving self.

When we were young we had little say about what we took in and what we didn't. We were sponges. Things came in and out of our boundaries without our say. Seeds were planted within us, many of which have not served us whatsoever.

Today, however, you choose what you take in and what you don't. You choose what seeds get planted within you, and in turn, what fruits are born from those seeds.

Get creative. Find an image. If you can see it you can be it.

Let not a man guard his dignity, but let his dignity guard him.
—Ralph Waldo Emerson

DAY 181
CREATE SOME NEW TRADITIONS

Have you been doing to yourself exactly what was done to you? Have you been blaming, shaming, judging, limiting, and disempowering yourself, heaping upon yourself the same discouraging messages you received in the past? If you didn't like it then, why are you still doing it today?

It makes perfect sense. It's not a choice; it's an automatic reaction. We take over where our histories left off. Until we learn better, we do things exactly the same way, treating ourselves today the way we were treated then.

But today is a new day. And it's time to create some new traditions. Think about the life you want to live. Then think about the habits that will get you there.

Having the life you've never had means doing some things you've never done.

We are what we repeatedly do. Excellence, then, is not an act, but a habit.
—Aristotle

DAY 182
CHOOSE AGAIN

When you are heading down a negative path, choose again. When you have made a choice that isn't working out, choose again. When you find yourself choosing self-defeating thoughts, choose again.

These words *choose again* remind us we are not victims of our circumstances, hostages to previous choices, or prisoners of our own thinking. It is possible to do an about-face. It's possible to turn around.

Give yourself permission to choose again. Change course when you need to. Remind yourself this is a viable option. Hear yourself say, "Choose again."

Your choices shape who you are. The doors you open and close each day determine the life you live. Be prepared to make adjustments along the way.

Choices are the hinges of destiny.
—Pythagoras

DAY 183
BLOW YOUR OWN MIND

Any day is a good day to do something different, to wake yourself up, and to tug your own chain.

How wonderful it is that we have the ability to transform ourselves and our lives. Each day we have the power to turn a corner—to create a new beginning. No matter our present experience, hope is never lost, because as humans, we have a profound capacity for change.

Surprise yourself. Create a sense of freshness in life. Look for ways to shake things up.

Go ahead. Blow your own mind.

It's a great thing when you realize you
still have the ability to surprise yourself.
—Lester Burnham

DAY 184
BE OPEN TO EVERYTHING

Be open to all experience—not only what you "think" you want.

Many of us over-script our lives. We attach ourselves to certain outcomes, feeling dismayed and defeated when our expectations are not met. We want what's comfortable and expected. When we don't get it, we don't know what to do with ourselves.

But what about the moments we couldn't possibly script? What about unexpected outcomes and unforeseen treasures? What about the meaning we find in the messiest of life experiences, the peace we find in the presence of pain, and the gratitude we find in grief?

There is beauty in surprises. There is significance in the unplanned and unexpected, however uncomfortable these may be. It's in the most unscripted of moments that we do some of our best living.

Don't close yourself off. Don't rob life of its richness. Be hungry and open to it all.

Constant development is the law of life, and a man
who always tries to maintain his dogmas in order to
appear consistent drives himself into a false position.
—Mohandas K. Gandhi

DAY 185
THINK POSITIVELY

A distorted belief system is toxic. It creates and perpetuates a battle within, as we live in reaction to our own negativity. We resist. We defend. We rationalize. We excuse. We project negativity onto others. We do anything and everything to cope with that toxicity inside of us—that is until we rewrite the script.

You are actually allergic to negativity. Your system has been fighting against it, hence that internal battle. You aren't meant to think poorly of yourself, and something is wrong if you do. Self-defeating thinking isn't natural.

Think what it would be like to stop fighting against your own belief system, to have your beliefs aligned with who you are, with your inherent worth and value. It's what you were meant to believe to begin with.

Get into the flow. Think positively.

A pessimist sees the difficulty in every opportunity;
an optimist sees the opportunity in every difficulty.
—Winston Churchill

DAY 186
SPEAK UP

Do you tend to hit the mute button on your life? Do you quiet yourself, lest others feel put out by you? Do you play small out of fear of coming off too big?

At one time we might have felt we needed to silence ourselves. So we mute ourselves today because we felt muted early on. But in doing so, we perpetrate against ourselves the very same patterns of abandonment and neglect. We invite our past into our present and suffer because of it.

Watch out for taking over where your history left off. Stop falling down on the job of being who you are. Stand up and be noticed. Announce yourself.

Have a voice in this life.

Never be bullied into silence. Never allow yourself to be made a victim.
Accept no one's definition of your life, but define yourself.
—Harvey S. Firestone

DAY 187
REFINE YOURSELF

We started out fine…then we got defined…now we're getting refined. I've always loved that saying.

You came into this life worthy, precious, and valuable. It's the truth of who you are and who you have always been.

But even though you started out fine, your world might have told you something different, making you feel anything but okay. Perhaps you have been living out negative messages ever since, perpetuating the same painful identity that was handed to you.

Whatever the world has said about you doesn't have to stick. Labels can be peeled off. You know how you came into this world, and you can get back to that truth at any time.

Refine yourself. Get down to being you.

As a man thinketh in his heart, so is he.
—James Allen

DAY 188
LIVE IN THE MIDDLE

Both the good times and the bad times have meaning. What we learn from each enlightens how we show up today.

What do we learn during the high times of life? We learn that life is abundant, that there is much for which to be grateful, that there is indeed a Universe conspiring for our good, and that things can and do work out. We learn that we are blessed.

What do we learn from the low times? We learn that there is strength in weakness, that there is peace in the presence of pain, that we are stronger than we think, and that we are resilient. We learn to persevere. We learn to keep the faith.

Life is full of peaks and valleys. But you need not wait for the high times to find happiness. And you don't have to live in fear of the lows. Whatever comes your way is there to enlighten you.

Life is not lived in extremes. Most of it exists somewhere in between. So find meaning in the middle ground.

It's where you spend most of your time anyway.

You have to take the good with the bad, smile with the sad, love what you've got and remember what you had, always forgive, but never forget, learn from your mistakes, but never regret. People change. Things go wrong. Just remember…life goes on.
—Author unknown

DAY 189
MOVE ON

Are you holding on to something that isn't serving you? Is it time to let go?

We fool ourselves into thinking that holding on works for us. We cling to people, to patterns and habits, to familiar thoughts and opinions, to old reactions, to control…even to painful memories and resentments. We tell ourselves they provide security.

Holding on only keeps us hostage to what was. It colors the present and impedes what can be. True power is found in letting go.

No more keeping yourself in a holding pattern. Choose to move forward instead.

The great thing in the world is not so much where we stand,
as in what direction we are moving.
—Oliver Wendell Holmes

DAY 190
PUSH THE PAST INTO THE PAST

Watch out for inviting your past into your present. Push the patterns that don't work for you—and haven't worked for you—into the past.

What this means is, when talking—even thinking—about personal tendencies that have not served you, put them into the past tense. "In the past I've been…." "I used to be…." "I have tended to…." Do this even if the past was literally yesterday.

Semantics mean everything. If we keep inviting into the present these negative patterns, where is the room for growth?

Today is a new day, and the perspective you adopt matters. How you motivate yourself determines how you feel and how you act.

Inspire yourself. Empower yourself. And by all means, push the past into the past.

When I let go of what I am, I become what I might be.
—Lao Tzu

DAY 191
LET GO OF THE FAMILIAR

We seem to cling to the very things that hurt us. It's one of our more destructive human tendencies. We hold on to the familiar, however harmful the familiar might be.

We cling to well-known thoughts, feelings, and behaviors. We cling to regret, remorse, and resentment. We cling to people, relationships, and patterns of engagement. The bottom line is that we are negatively attached.

We are bonded to the things that have been damaging. We are used to them. Better the enemy we know than something unknown, we think. We have no idea how good it will feel to break free from those attachments.

Take a look at what you're holding on to and why. The familiar could be stealing your spirit.

We would rather be ruined than changed.
We would rather die in our dread
Than climb the cross of the present
And let our illusions die.
—W. H. Auden

DAY 192
KILL SOME SACRED COWS

A sacred cow is a cow or a bull looked at with sincere reverence. Figuratively speaking, it's something considered immune from question or criticism. A sacred cow might be a belief—one we consider exempt from doubt or debate.

Often, our sacred cows are self-defeating and toxic. They drag us down. But we cling to them nonetheless.

I should always be happy. It's not okay to make mistakes. I have to earn my worth and value. I need to be approved of by others. I have to be good. Life is meant to keep me comfortable.

Maybe you've been worshipping some sacred cows. They're not serving you, but because they're familiar, they're strangely comfortable. They're all you've ever known. Abandon them nonetheless.

It's time to kill some sacred cows. They're nothing but false gods anyway.

Change your thoughts, and you change your world.
—Norman Vincent Peale

DAY 193
GIVE YOUR EXPERIENCES MEANING

You are not defined by your history. Nor are you the sum total of your present experiences. You are the measure of how you respond to it all.

To a large extent, life simply happens to us. From profound themes in our past, such as childhood trauma, to the small, day-to-day frustrations and setbacks we all experience, there is much that is beyond our control. There is much about which we have no say. What we do have a say in is how we deal with it.

We can choose to react. We can be resentful and remorseful. We can be victims. We can take our anger out on loved ones. We can pay negativity forward by showing up negatively.

Or we can choose a different path. We can make a decision to learn from life experience, to grow from what has happened, to look at life as our teacher, and to find empowerment in each and every life lesson.

It isn't your circumstances that define you. It is you within them. It's you who gives your experiences meaning. You determine their significance.

Watch out for over-identifying with your story. It's not what happens to you; it's what you do with it.

People are not disturbed by things, but by the view they take of them.
—Epictetus

DAY 194
FOCUS ON WHAT MATTERS

On our journey to personal freedom, we let go of a lot. One thing we let go of is our attachment to things that don't matter.

Each of us has frustrations. If we nurture them, they grow. Shift attention elsewhere and they lose their power. We can then put our power where it counts.

Liberate yourself by letting go of the unimportant. Stop sweating the small stuff. Stop majoring in the minors.

Focus instead on the things that matter.

Life is thickly sown with thorns, and I know no other remedy than to pass quickly through them. The longer we dwell on our misfortunes, the greater is their power to harm us.
—Voltaire

DAY 195
DREAM

Do you allow yourself to dream, or have you forgotten how? Do you negate your dreams before they stand a chance? Do you tell yourself they're unrealistic, improbable, and frivolous?

Dreaming isn't a luxury available only to some. It's available to each and every one of us. It's our personal right. If it feels unnatural to dream, it needs to become natural again.

Let yourself visualize. Allow yourself to explore, put yourself into wonderful places, and try on a life you love. You will draw motivation from your dreams. Your visualizations will propel you forward.

It takes courage to dream, especially when you have lost the ability to do so. But you can liberate yourself and learn to dream again. You can reclaim this basic and pleasurable right.

Your dreams are the expression of your spirit. Don't limit them with practicality. The power isn't in what you achieve. The power is in the dreaming itself.

Whatever you do, dream.

Cherish your visions and your dreams as they are the children of your soul, the blueprints of your ultimate achievements.
—Napoleon Hill

DAY 196
CREATE YOUR NEW NORMAL

Your journey to personal freedom is about creating a new normal, a new baseline, and a whole new sense of the familiar.

The old ways might be dysfunctional, but they're also familiar. Self-defeating emotional, mental, and behavioral patterns have carved a well-worn groove. Maybe we are used to limiting our potential. It's what we know. And we tend to be creatures of habit.

It's possible nonetheless to create a new sense of the familiar. It's possible to create a fresh template for how we show up in this life and for how we think, feel, and behave.

It's a wonderful thing that, while we think we know normal, we can create a whole new normal. We can learn an entirely new way of showing up in this life, one that over time will become the familiar path—the more comfortable way to be.

With dedication and commitment, self-care and wellbeing will become the standard. Dysfunction will be the aberration.

Welcome to your new normal.

Today is the first day of the rest of your life.
—Author unknown

DAY 197
CHOOSE CHANGE OVER FEAR

Do you freeze up at the prospect of change? Do you cling to security at the expense of personal growth?

Change is happening all the time. We don't have a choice about it. What we do have a choice about is how we perceive change, whether we oppose or favor it, and whether we seek it out or fight hard against it. Fear tells us to resist change. Faith says to embrace it.

Instead of opposing change, choose it and welcome it. As you do, you will find you're more flexible than you thought. You will discover new pathways and possibilities. You will achieve outcomes you never dreamed of before.

Don't let fear hold you back from a life you could love. Lean into change and grow.

To exist is to change, to change is to mature,
to mature is to go on creating oneself endlessly.
—Henri Bergson

DAY 198
BREAK FREE

Many of us are rules-bound. The rules come from messages we received early on in life. They come from expectations. They come from everything we have been told about who we should and shouldn't be. They come from outside of us.

Over time, these rules become internalized, and we find ourselves living restricted, self-regulated lives. We become cautious and rigid. We box ourselves in and limit our joy. We tell ourselves it isn't okay to be who we are. We might not remember how we got this way; we just know we feel confined and constricted.

Life isn't lived by rules. Life is lived by letting go, breaking free from restrictions, and letting yourself be.

Stop ruling things out—especially who you are and what you love.

If I'd observed all the rules, I'd never have gotten anywhere.
—Marilyn Monroe

DAY 199
BE OPEN TO POSSIBILITY

Watch out for locking yourself into one way of being. Be careful about telling yourself there's only one way to live your life, to find satisfaction, to follow your dreams, and to make yourself happy. Thinking this might be keeping you stuck.

If you've been pigeon-holing yourself into one path, into one way of doing things, into a role or a goal that isn't a fit, you've likely been making yourself a little bit crazy.

Be flexible with yourself. There are many different paths you can take in this life. There are many routes to fulfillment. If one doesn't work, you can take another. You can change course when you need to.

Don't miss the options and opportunities before you. There are many ways to live this life.

Life is a great big canvas, and you
should throw all the paint on it you can.
—Danny Kaye

DAY 200
ANTICIPATE THE GOOD

Worry does an excellent job of predicting the negative. It's great at identifying and ruminating over potential problems. What it doesn't do is solve them.

We seem to think our worry serves a preventative purpose. In planning for the worst—in trying to mitigate future pain and discomfort—we tell ourselves we are being productive. The truth is, there is nothing productive about worry.

Worry backfires. Worry saps our energy and drains our life force. Worry doesn't eliminate future troubles; it only robs today of its joy. It keeps us in a fruitless cycle of fearful rumination.

If you want to do something constructive, let go of worry. Occupy your mind with positive thoughts. Use your energy wisely. Choose a focal point that actually works for you.

If you're going to anticipate anything, anticipate the good.

When I look back on all these worries, I remember the story of the old man who said on his deathbed that he had had a lot of trouble in his life, most of which had never happened.
—Winston Churchill

DAY 201
TRANSFORM YOUR EMOTIONAL ENERGY

Emotional healing involves learning to transform emotional energy.

In martial arts they talk of transforming an opponent's energy. The martial artist is said to use the energy of the opponent to his or her desired end. We can choose to use the emotional energy around us and within us for our own self-determined purposes. Even other people's negativity can be used for our good.

Emotions are made of energy—and energy always changes form. No feeling lasts forever. Even so, you need not wait around for emotional energy to change. You can shift the energy. Anyone who has ever turned grief into gratitude, pain into peace, frustration into acceptance, or negativity into positivity knows this to be true.

You get to decide how to use whatever emotion you're feeling or whatever energy you have picked up. Transforming emotions and the energy associated with them is fundamental to emotional health. All emotions can be used for our enlightenment. It's our choice.

No emotion is ever wasted if you harness it for a purpose.

One ought to hold on to one's heart;
for if one lets it go, one soon loses control of the head too.
—Friedrich Nietzsche

DAY 202
SPIRAL UPWARD

Spiral Dynamics says that humans are not fixed, but rather highly flexible and adaptable. We have the potential for constant growth and enlightenment, developing increasingly complex ideas about our world as we make our way through life.

You too can spiral upward. It's about staying open and thirsty for understanding. During the most trying times of life, you can choose to learn, grow, and become richer for your experiences. You can challenge previously held beliefs and stretch yourself in ways you had never known possible.

Take loss, for example. If you face your grief head on—if you walk directly through it with a teachable spirit—it need not paralyze you. You can evolve in the most profound ways right in the midst of loss.

Seek enlightenment and your life will be an upward spiral.

Experience is not what happens to a man.
It is what a man does with what happens to him.
—Aldous Huxley

DAY 203
RELEASE RIGHTNESS AND WRONGNESS

You don't have to figure out who is right or wrong. You only need to know what does or doesn't work for you.

This concept rocked my foundation when I first heard it.

Our attachment to rightness keeps us stuck in reactivity. Liberation comes from letting go. It comes from releasing ourselves from the bondage of true or false, good or bad, and right or wrong. It comes from remembering what does and doesn't matter.

Instead of getting embroiled in mental debates and power struggles, just honor your own reality. Know that it's valid because it's yours. Sometimes all you need to say is, "That doesn't work for me." It's a perfectly legitimate statement.

The next time you find yourself clinging to that winner-loser mindset, take a deep breath and remind yourself, "I don't have to figure out who is right or wrong; I only need to know what does or doesn't work for me."

It's very liberating.

Out beyond ideas of wrongdoing and rightdoing, there is a field.
I'll meet you there.
—Rumi

DAY 204
MOVE THROUGH FEAR

Doing what frightens us brings blessings. Facing fear head on and choosing to move through it is how we build a life we love—a life we can feel good about.

As you walk through the discomfort of fear, as you confront the negative thoughts driving it, and as you engage in the very things that scare you, you'll find they're not so scary after all. You'll realize you're stronger than you think. You'll feel a weight lifted. You'll feel empowered. You'll move closer to your goals.

Fear is unavoidable. It's part of the human experience. But how you choose to handle your fear is entirely within your power. Get hungry for the gifts on the other side of it.

Walk through fear. Grow and gain faith in yourself. Watch as your life takes shape.

Never let the fear of striking out get in your way.
—Babe Ruth

DAY 205
LIVE LIFE FROM THE INSIDE OUT

We tend to do things backwards. We allow other people to tell us who we are and who we should be. We let our environments dictate how we show up. We allow outer circumstances to define our mindset and mood.

Letting externals determine internals is an unstable way to live. We feel good one minute, bad the next. Self-esteem is solid when we are on, weak when we are off. Our identity is secure when our environment is reinforcing us, shaky when it isn't. We feel peace when things are going smoothly, none when they are not.

Living from our core, on the other hand, offers a sense of permanence within—a stability of self. We know who we are. We hold on to our identity.

You are the expert on *you*. So don't let your world tell you who you are. Be internally directed, rather than externally driven.

It's the only way to go.

There are three things extremely hard:
steel, a diamond, and to know one's self.
—Benjamin Franklin

DAY 206
LET GO OF THE PAST

Do you allow your past to color your present? Do you invite feelings and experiences from your history into today? Does life feel like more of the same?

Whatever we have not yet resolved from our past only taints our present. It shapes our interpretation of current conditions. It feels like things will never change. But this isn't true. Our past is not our potential.

Stop replacing the present with the past. Stop contaminating today with yesterday. Put a period on your history, and give the present a chance.

If we open a quarrel between the past and the present,
we shall find we have lost the future.
—Winston Churchill

DAY 207
INVENTORY YOUR BELIEFS

Take an inventory of your belief system. Look for the contaminants within it. A belief system built in any way on trauma and wounding will become toxic to your wellbeing.

These negative mental intruders create resistance within. You want to move forward and be free, but harmful thoughts keep holding you back. They impede your ability to fully become who you are.

Make a decision to relate to yourself in a whole new way, no longer living out the remnants of past experiences. Choose what you think about yourself. Take over where your history left off by cleaning up your belief system where it needs cleaning up.

We learn what we live. But it's never too late to unlearn it!

The world we see that seems so insane is the result of a belief system that is not working. To perceive the world differently, we must be willing to change our belief system, let the past slip away, expand our sense of now, and dissolve the fear in our minds.
—William James

DAY 208
FREE YOURSELF WITH ACCEPTANCE

Do something totally radical: accept yourself.

Accepting yourself means loving yourself, being kind to yourself, and claiming all of who you are. It's treating yourself the way you know to treat others.

Now, however, comes the tougher part: stop criticizing yourself. Own your weaknesses, free from blame, shame, and self-judgment. Look yourself directly in the eye and accept yourself—fully.

This doesn't mean to sit back, resting in self-acceptance, not making every effort to grow and change—quite the contrary, in fact. This is about accepting yourself as a means to transformation.

One of the great paradoxes of personal growth is that in order to change certain things about ourselves, we need to first accept ourselves exactly as we are. No one evolves in an atmosphere of self-condemnation.

Liberate yourself with acceptance instead.

Accept yourself as you are.
Otherwise you will never see opportunity.
You will not feel free to move toward it;
you will feel you are not deserving.
—Maxwell Maltz

DAY 209
FOLLOW THROUGH

Determination. Tenacity. Stick-to-itiveness. This is how we get things done. This is how we make our dreams a reality.

How many times do you make promises to yourself, only to lose steam and end up discouraged? How often do you set out to improve yourself, but because of a lack of follow-through, you end up feeling even worse about yourself than before you started?

Incomplete dreams and unfinished ambitions damage faith in self. They erode self-respect. They become self-fulfilling prophecies. When we don't follow through, we feel badly about ourselves. And because we feel badly about ourselves, we don't follow through. It's a vicious cycle.

No more false starts. No more half measures. Set goals and complete them, however big or small they may be.

Your personal freedom depends on your ability to follow through.

We learn by doing.
—Aristotle

DAY 210
DROP THE FALSE GUILT

We all feel guilt. Much of the time we have just cause to feel it. But what about the times when there is no just cause at all?

Guilt is driven by the thought that we have acted outside our value system. It's that nagging and gnawing sensation in the gut that tells us we have broken our own moral code. Often the guilt we feel makes perfect sense. We have indeed departed from our core values. The guilt is authentic, and the healthy management of it is acknowledgment and amends.

But for many of us, guilt is a chronic condition. We feel guilty about virtually everything. We feel guilty about *being*. Guilt has become woven into who we are. This is often called false guilt.

The next time you feel guilt, ask yourself if you have actually stepped outside your value system. Have you earned the guilt you feel? Or are you feeling guilty simply because you've broken some old, self-limiting codes? Maybe you have stepped outside someone else's expectations. Maybe you're just used to feeling guilty. Maybe guilt is nothing but a bad habit.

Do a reality check on guilt. Lighten the load where you can by releasing what's false. You will be glad you did.

A guilty conscience never feels secure.
—Syrus

DAY 211
CREATE YOUR OWN MIRACLES

Amazing things happen when we change the way we look at things. A shift in attitude is nothing short of a miracle.

You are your own change agent. You get to choose your perspective. In turn, you choose how you experience and approach life. Only you know when you need that shift in perception. Only you know when change is needed.

In every moment you can shift your perception. In every moment you can see things through new eyes. Choose a new outlook, and create miracles in your life.

Shifting perception is nothing short of a miracle.

Miracles happen to those who believe in them.
—Bernard Berenson

DAY 212
CHOOSE FREEDOM OVER CONNECTION

There is an important balance we seek in life and in our relationships: between freedom and connection, between autonomy and intimacy. One without the other is unsatisfying in the long run. But one is actually a prerequisite for the other.

Needless to say, connectedness matters. Without it, we feel lonely and isolated. We were built for community, and we hunger for relationships.

Connection without freedom, however, doesn't work. We can lose ourselves to our relationships and end up defining ourselves through others.

In other words, your personal freedom is what matters most. Personal autonomy is essential to happiness and healthy relationships. You can't show up functionally if you are relating to others from a deficit within or placing intimacy above autonomy. A deep connection with self is the necessary starting point.

Get your freedom on board. Come to the table whole. Then let your relationships take shape accordingly.

Love yourself first and everything else falls into line.
You really have to love yourself to get anything done in this world.
—Lucille Ball

DAY 213
BE PATIENT. THE LESSONS WILL BE REVEALED.

Part of being human is the tendency to want to figure it all out. We want to know why we go through what we do. We want to see the good in the bad. We want to find the meaning in the turmoil. We want the lessons—and we want them now.

Each of us wants our experiences to have significance. We want them to make sense. Much of the time, however, we don't get the clarity we crave—at least not right away.

Then, as time passes and we get down the road a bit, we look back at those hard times with newfound insight and awareness. We see things we were not able to see before. We see the lessons. At last, we find the meaning.

Let go of the need to figure it all out. Be patient. The lessons will reveal themselves.

I am always ready to learn, although I do not always like being taught.
—Winston Churchill

DAY 214
ASK, WHAT DOES IT ALL MEAN?

On an almost nightly basis throughout my younger years, my father would stand at my bedroom door, lean against the door jamb, and ask, "Well, kid, what does it all mean?" The question always got me thinking. I've been thinking about it ever since.

A primary cause of stress is the absence of meaning in our lives. We walk around in the dark, unconscious about our true selves, disconnected with our worlds, and confused about the *whys* of life. We wonder what it all means.

Having wrestled with my father's question for years, I arrived at an answer I could feel good about.

The meaning of life is found in revealing and living your highest potential. It's about getting to know who you are and living in alignment with your true nature. It's being wide awake and fully alive, living a life of purpose. It's making every moment count.

Find your personal meaning of life by living in accordance with true self. Ask not: "Who do I want to be?" Ask: "How can I be who I am?"

Man's ideal state is realized when he has fulfilled the purpose for which he is born. And what is it that reason demands of him? Something very easy—that he live in accordance with his own nature.
—Seneca

DAY 215
TRUST YOURSELF

All too often we put our peace and our power in other people's hands. We make our internal state contingent upon how others show up.

When we believe we can trust someone, we give ourselves permission to relax, ease up, and simply be. We find comfort and security in the fact that we can bank on another to show up a certain way. We allow ourselves peace.

But making our internal state the measure of other people's trustworthiness—or lack thereof—is risky business. Needing others to show up a certain way in order to feel peace means our sense of security is here one minute and potentially gone the next.

People please us. People disappoint us. At times they deserve our trust, at times they don't. At times they meet our expectations, at times they won't. The most important person you can count on is *you*.

Your security and serenity need not be contingent upon others—only upon you. Knowing you can count on yourself—that you will always come to your own assistance, and that even if someone breaks your trust, you will be okay—is where peace is found.

At the end of the day, you need to know you can count on *you*.

A man who doesn't trust himself can never truly trust anyone else.
—Cardinal de Retz

DAY 216
SPREAD LOVE

Share love and you will feel love. Give it away and you will get it back. Love creates love. That's the way it works.

If you're feeling a lack of love in your life, there's a solution. Become a more loving presence in your world. Reach out, extend yourself, and give away what you want in return. It won't take long to find that the energy you put out there attracts more of the same.

Set out today with the intention of spreading love. Be the love you want to experience.

Love grows by giving.
The love we give away is the only love we keep.
The only way to retain love is to give it away.
—Elbert Hubbard

DAY 217
REMEMBER HOW FAR YOU HAVE COME

"I may not be where I want to be yet, but I sure as heck am not where I was." I've always loved this affirmation.

On our journey to personal freedom, we have to learn to be in between. In fact, life is all about being in between.

But we get so uncomfortable with this place. We don't like living in the gray. We want black or white. We want certainty. We want change. We want to cross that finish line.

The in-between place is actually the most fertile ground of all—if we can make peace with it. The in-between place keeps us hungry. The in-between place is where we grow. We have goals in sight and strive for change, but we are not in a hurry. We allow ourselves to be in transition. We are in the process of being changed.

Being in between is about acknowledging how much we have already grown. It's also knowing there is more growth ahead. By honoring what we have already accomplished, we are motivated for even more.

You are your way. You are on the path. So be patient. You may not be where you want to be, but you sure as heck are not where you were!

It's not so much that we're afraid of change or so in love with the old ways, but it's that place in between that we fear. It's like being between trapezes. It's Linus when his blanket is in the dryer. There's nothing to hold on to.
—Marilyn Ferguson

DAY 218
LIVE WHOLLY

We always hear that we should live life to the fullest, that we should make the most of every day. But what exactly does this mean? The answer is up to you.

Maybe it's about productivity and purpose. Perhaps it's fun and enjoyment. It might be about gratitude and rejoicing in the little things. Maybe it's being with people you love. Or it could be a day of actively pursuing your dreams.

Choosing to live life to the fullest holds many blessings. By committing yourself to living wholly, you will embrace and appreciate each day. You will prioritize and accomplish things. You will be intentional about how you show up. You will feel empowered and in charge of your daily experience.

Live life to the fullest. Celebrate the gift of today.

And in the end, it's not the years in your life that count.
It's the life in your years.
—Abraham Lincoln

DAY 219
LIVE WHAT YOU LOVE

Are you living a life you love? A life you feel good about? Are you engaging your passions and interests? Or do you see fun as frivolous? Something only afforded the young?

Fun isn't frivolous, and it isn't just for kids. Growing up doesn't mean you divorce your spontaneity and playfulness. You just have to be more deliberate about them.

Let yourself be lighthearted. Maintain enjoyment throughout your life. Give yourself permission to play, to explore, and to pursue what you love. Weave delight into all you do, not just into your spare time.

Set the intention to live a life you love. Now hold that intention.

One day your life will flash before your eyes.
Make sure it's worth watching.
—Author unknown

DAY 220
LET GO OF THE TIMETABLES

You're right on time.

It's a reassuring thought, isn't it? Many of us, however, assume we know where we should and shouldn't be in life at any given time. We have set expectations, and they get us in trouble.

Your journey doesn't follow some universal timetable, and your growth process is as unique as you are. Stop questioning things, and go with the flow. There is no serenity in stumbling over yesterday or fussing about tomorrow. The only truly significant moment is right here, right now.

The next time you're yearning to retrieve lost time—or wanting to speed things along—just take a deep breath, exhale, and remind yourself *you're right on time*.

Feel the comfort it brings.

Having spent the better part of my life trying either to relive the past
or experience the future before it arrives, I have come to believe
that in between these two extremes is peace.
—Author unknown

DAY 221
INVEST IN THE NOW

We can get so paralyzed by decision-making—crippled by the choices we think we have to make…and have to make now. Should I stay or go? Should I take action or do nothing? Should I follow this path or that one?

We can't seem to make up our minds. So we ruminate. We cogitate. We seek input from others, taking surveys about what we should or shouldn't do. We expend endless energy trying to figure it all out. However, as hard as we try to force the issue, we remain hostage to indecision.

Being stuck in indecision is like being in a holding pattern, half present in our own lives. But we don't have to stay this way. We simply need to break out of the analysis paralysis, start listening to our inner voice, and allow enlightenment to evolve.

If you feel incapacitated by a decision before you, it might not be time to make it. Just honor your feelings, plug into today, and let your path naturally take shape.

Invest in the now and clarity will come.

Do something. If it works, do more of it. If it doesn't, do something else.
—Franklin D. Roosevelt

DAY 222
GIVE YOURSELF A DO-OVER

Today is a good day to do things differently. It's a good day to come to your own assistance and give yourself precisely what you've wanted and needed all along.

As an adult, only you can parent yourself. This is bad news and good news. The bad news is, if you are falling down on the job, it is your responsibility and yours alone. The good news is, if you are falling down on the job, it is your responsibility and yours alone!

In other words, you have the power within yourself to come to your own assistance. You have the power to encourage your own growth and create your own happiness.

You might not have received the healthiest messages in the past by those whose responsibility it was to parent you, but today you get to do things differently. Today you can take over where your history left off—not by repeating the patterns of the past, but by breaking them.

If you haven't been doing the self-parenting job you know you need to do, give yourself a do-over. It's never too late to dote on that precious child within.

*The image of myself which I try to create in my own mind in order that
I may love myself is very different from the image which I try to
create in the minds of others in order that they may love me.*
—W. H. Auden

DAY 223
FOLLOW YOUR WHOLENESS

What would it be like to live a life where you use your gifts, talents, and interests? Where you make the most of all of you?

Many of us go only to the places where certain aspects of ourselves allow us to go. We give ourselves limited permission to *be*, engaging only parts of ourselves and realizing only some of our aspirations.

We tell ourselves we should be this kind of person or that. In doing so, we discourage our dreams. We compromise.

If you were to listen to your heart—if you were to go within and ask what kind of life your soul wants to live—what would it look like?

Stop limiting your options to those that seem logical and reasonable. Stop boxing yourself in. Go where your wholeness calls you to go.

Life is either a daring adventure or nothing at all.
—Helen Keller

DAY 224
CULTIVATE YOUR DREAMS

All too often we latch onto other people's agendas, desires, and dreams. Because of it, we remain hungry, dissatisfied, and ill-suited for our own lives, like square pegs trying to fit into round holes.

Stop hijacking other people's dreams and make a decision to cultivate your own instead. As you do, life will begin to flow. Energy will find its right direction. Your dreams will begin to take shape.

Get to know yourself. Think about what makes you *you*. Take stock of your passions and talents—of what lights you up and gets you going. Give yourself permission to have your own unique vision, allowing your dreams to emerge from your core.

Watch as things start to happen.

Go confidently in the direction of your dreams.
Live the life you have imagined.
—Henry David Thoreau

DAY 225
CHOOSE THOUGHTS YOU LIKE

We think thoughts we don't even like. We then wonder why our lives are not running smoothly.

Early on in life, we had limited power over what we started telling ourselves, and over the beliefs we formed. We were sponges, absorbing messages from our environment. We formed a life script accordingly.

Today you get to choose what you think. You get to choose thoughts that encourage and empower, that comfort and nurture, and that make you feel good.

Perhaps it's time to clean up your thinking. This time, pick thoughts you actually like.

A man is but the product of his thoughts. What he thinks, he becomes.
—Mahatma Gandhi

DAY 226
BREAK THE SELF-CRITICISM HABIT

On the road to personal freedom, self-compassion might be the most important life skill we can develop.

Self-compassion is our refuge. It's our safety and comfort, our buffer against what could otherwise rattle, distract, and discourage us. It's the loving motivation behind all we do. It's our key to liberation.

When you stop criticizing yourself, you can start loving yourself. When you stop judging, ranking, and comparing yourself to others, and when you lean fully into who you are, loving yourself no matter what, you are at last free. Kindness and compassion are turned inward.

Exhale into who you are. Embrace your true self. Be patient and loving with yourself. Your life will change as you do.

If you're going to break any habit, break the self-criticism habit.

Life, I fancy, would very often be insupportable,
but for the luxury of self-compassion.
—George R. Gissing

DAY 227
BE PREPARED

We all have dry spells. We all hit plateaus along the way. At times like these, it can feel as if we are standing still. It doesn't mean we are.

As long as we stay inspired and continue exposing ourselves to the things that stimulate and motivate us, we are indeed progressing—even if it seems we are not. We are preparing for our next growth spurt. We are readying ourselves for change.

Sometimes life feels like survival. And getting through the dry spells can be hard. But as long as you continue feeding yourself inspiration, the feeling of inertia won't last long. Put one foot in front of the other, and before you know it, you will feel that momentum building again.

You never know what's right around the corner.

I think I can, I think I can.
—The Little Engine That Could

DAY 228
TURN FEELINGS INTO INTENTIONS

Uncomfortable emotions have a way of stopping us dead in our tracks. We deny them, run from them, stuff them, and medicate them. But it doesn't have to be this way. We can channel discomfort into motivation and purpose. Even the most painful emotions can become our intentions.

What don't you like about your life? What do the feelings you have about these things tell you about yourself? How can you use this information for your own betterment, turning what you don't want into what you do want?

Your feelings need not hold you hostage any longer. Your feelings can motivate you in powerful ways if you learn from them and choose how to use their energy. You don't have to stay discouraged and dissatisfied. You don't have to remain so hungry.

No emotion is ever for nothing. Let it speak to you. It always has something to say.

Doubt is a pain too lonely to know that faith is his twin brother.
—Khalil Gibran

DAY 229
NURTURE YOUR PASSION

We often judge our passions. We think they have to play out in tangible ways in order to be worthy. If we can't see clear outcomes for our passions, we starve and deny them.

Perhaps you have a passion for writing, but you don't see yourself as talented enough to be published. You can discount this passion, labeling it impractical and improbable. Or you can engage it, regardless of any measurable outcome, valuing passion for passion's sake and enjoying the process. It's your choice.

Anything that ignites you defines you, and all passion is precious and deserving. So stop smothering it with practicality. You never know how it might play out.

Engage what you love, and let go of the rest.

You will need to find your passion. Don't give up on finding it because then all you're doing is waiting for the Reaper.
—Randy Pausch

DAY 230
LIVE YOUR REFRAMES

If you want to change the way you look at things, start by reframing the negative messages you've been telling yourself. One thought at a time, transform a disempowering mindset into an empowering one. In time, your entire worldview will change.

"I can't stand myself" becomes "I am learning to love myself." "I am stuck" becomes "I am growing and changing every day." "I can't do anything right" becomes "I am perfectly imperfect" or "I love and accept myself."

We are not born with negative thoughts. We learn them. Then we live them. They end up shaping the way we experience our worlds.

In terms of our hope for change, this is good news. Since our negative beliefs were learned, we have the power to change them. We have the power to create new thoughts, learn these thoughts well, live them out, and shape a whole new existence for ourselves.

If you're tired of seeing yourself through a painful, self-deprecating lens and are ready for a powerful change, you know what to do. Put some new thoughts into practice, live these reframes, and watch your life transform.

If you hear a voice within you say "you cannot paint,"
then by all means paint, and that voice will be silenced.
—Vincent Van Gogh

DAY 231
LET GO TO LET IN

The Buddhists say our spiritual path is about non-clinging—that true liberation comes through non-attachment to our thoughts and feelings. And it's not just the Buddhists.

We let go of a lot in order to be available to life. We let go of anger, resentment, doubt, frustration, pain over the past, fear about the future…anything that could otherwise consume and preoccupy. If we don't let go, we carry these things around, and they drag us down.

While it's important to honor our thoughts and feelings, we can also take them too seriously and allow them to linger too long. Instead of allowing things to flow, we hold on to our attachments, thinking there is power in doing so.

Non-clinging is a truly spiritual practice. By releasing our attachments—by opening up and letting go—we can be fully present and available to life. We are wide open to receive.

You have to let go to let in.

God is always trying to give good things to us,
but our hands are too full to receive them.
—St. Augustine

DAY 232
JUST DO IT

When you think about it, *try* is a pretty weak word. I'll try to get it done. I'll try to follow through. I'll try to be better.

There's a lot behind that one little word. Try says we are not quite sure we can accomplish what we say we will. We are not convinced of our ability to make assurances. We don't believe in ourselves. Not fully.

Try is noncommittal. We resist promising anything, at least not with any certainty. We either lack faith in ourselves or we don't want the accountability that comes with making a commitment. So we say, "I'll try." It's flabby. It's feeble.

Make a promise instead. Tell yourself you can and will do whatever it is you used to say you would try to do. Really sink your teeth into personal change.

Try might be moving in the right direction, but it's not good enough.

> *You are the person who has to decide*
> *Whether you'll do it or toss it aside.*
> *You are the person who makes up your mind*
> *Whether you'll lead or will linger behind,*
> *Whether you'll try for the goal that's afar,*
> *Or just be contented to stay where you are.*
> —Edgar A. Guest

DAY 233
STAND BY YOUR FEELINGS

Each of us has a right to our feelings, whatever they might be and whenever we might have them. We can't be truly free until we embrace this simple truth.

Maybe we learned early on that it wasn't okay to feel certain feelings. As a result, we feel apologetic about feeling them. Perhaps we never learned to express our feelings responsibly, and because of the unbecoming way we convey them, we feel guilty about having them at all. But none of this means we have to apologize for what we feel.

Having a right to your feelings isn't about expressing them however you choose. There's a right way and a wrong way to share what you feel. Anger doesn't have to be expressed as rage. Fear doesn't have to come out as control. Pain doesn't have to be painful to others. However, when managed and expressed appropriately, your feelings are more than acceptable, and it's healthy to express them.

Stop turning your back on precisely what makes you human.

Never apologize for showing feeling.
When you do so, you apologize for the truth.
—Benjamin Disraeli

DAY 234
GIVE YOURSELF CORRECTIVE EXPERIENCES

Each of us hungers for experiences that will make right what hasn't felt right within. We want to correct the hurts of our past. We hunger for wholeness. We hunger for healing.

What we often underestimate is the power we have to restore our own wellbeing and give ourselves these corrective experiences. We overlook our own healing potential—and it's time we do something about it.

If you've been afraid of speaking up for yourself, then grab opportunities to show up and speak up. See that you can have a voice.

If you've tended to play small, then start playing bigger. See what it feels like to claim your right size.

If you've doubted yourself, then set a goal and accomplish it. See what it feels like to keep your word to yourself.

You hold the keys to healing some age-old wounds and replacing those assumptions with new self-conceptions. Today you get to turn things around.

Give yourself those restorative moments as only you can.

Healing is a matter of time, but it is
sometimes also a matter of opportunity.
—Hippocrates

DAY 235
FREE THE IMPERFECTION WITHIN

Do you embrace your imperfection, or do you fight against it? Do you love yourself in the face of failure, or do you resist your own fallibility, refusing to give in to the very thing that makes you human?

Freedom is more than liberating the greatness within. It is more than power, victory, and strength. Personal freedom is liberating all of who we are. This includes our imperfection.

"I'm human." "I'm perfectly imperfect." "There's my humanness showing again." I feel emancipated each time I say these things.

Embracing imperfection means we acknowledge weakness where there is weakness. We admit failure where there is failure. We own the good and the not-so-good, the power and the powerlessness. We meet ourselves in our humanness, and we love ourselves in that place.

We can't pick and choose our freedom. We can't free only parts of who we are. It doesn't work that way. We have to liberate it all.

Free the imperfection within. That's true emancipation.

Freedom is not worth having if it does not connote freedom to err.
—Mahatma Gandhi

DAY 236
SAVOR THOSE "LIFE IS GOOD" MOMENTS

We all have them. You know, those moments when you stop, pause, and take stock of just how wonderful life actually is. Those times when you say to yourself, "Life is gooood."

Give these moments the attention and significance they deserve. Honor them. Express gratitude for them. Write them down. Share them with someone else. Whatever you do, make sure you savor them.

The more you do, the more they'll seem to happen.

Life is good when we think it's good. Life is bad when we don't think.
—Doug Horton

DAY 237
CUT THE APRON STRINGS

What's keeping you from stepping boldly into today? What vestiges of your history are holding you back? What outdated self-conceptions?

On our path to personal freedom, we have to confront the negative ties we have to our histories. We need to take a hard look at how we have remained loyal to the very themes that have disempowered us. We have to ask ourselves why we remain hitched to pain and faithful to negativity.

Why do we hold on, especially when letting go would be so liberating?

Cut the cord. Free yourself. Break out of the themes that bind and betray you. Those apron strings have been keeping you from becoming who you were destined to be.

There is nothing virtuous about remaining loyal to a painful past. That loyalty could be killing you.

> *What you need to know about the past is that*
> *no matter what has happened, it has all worked together*
> *to bring you to this very moment. And this is the moment*
> *you can choose to make everything new. Right now.*
> —Author unknown

DAY 238
CHOOSE WHAT YOU PUT IN THE FOREGROUND

What we focus on determines our overall life experience. Where we put our attention, we put our energy. And where we put energy, we create outcomes.

Life is both light and dark, good and bad. Where you put your focus is a life-defining choice. Is your perspective serving you or hurting you?

Focus on what's present in your life rather than what's missing. Draw your attention to abundance rather than deprivation. Put your values front and center and focus on what's important. Magnify the positive.

What you choose to put in your personal foreground matters. Choose wisely.

> *He is a wise man who does not grieve for the things*
> *which he has not, but rejoices for those which he has.*
> —Epictetus

DAY 239
BE PREPARED. OLD WAYS DIE HARD.

You want change. You're hungry for it. You're working toward it. Even so, change doesn't happen overnight.

However you're living, it's likely you've been living this way a long time. You've carved some well-worn grooves of behavior. It will take time to turn things around.

Life isn't linear. Neither is change. As we marshal in the new, the old ways will resurface. Don't be surprised or discouraged when they do. Be patient, press on, and maintain your tenacity and stick-to-itiveness. The old ways aren't going to give up the throne that easily.

If we are facing in the right direction,
all we have to do is keep on walking.
—Buddhist saying

DAY 240
ASK, WHY NOT ME?

A "why me?" attitude never serves us. Singling ourselves out in this way can be self-destructive.

Our "why me?" attitude typically shows up during adversity. *Why did this happen to me? Why am I so unlucky? Why did I deserve this?*

Our "why me?" mindset can affect how we see potential good things as well. *Why would things work out as I want? Why would I be so blessed? Why would I deserve it?*

In this life you will experience sorrow, disappointment, and painful surprises. You will also experience joy, success, and unexpected good fortune. It's all part of the human journey. You are just as likely as anyone to be exposed to both good and bad.

Stop setting yourself apart with a "why me?" attitude. Watch that terminal uniqueness. You are no more deserving of pain and no less deserving of pleasure than anyone else.

Instead of asking, "Why me?" ask, "Why not me?"

A true man never frets about his place in the world, but just slides into it by the gravitation of his nature, and swings there as easily as a star.
—Edwin Hubbel Chapin

DAY 241
BREATHE A LITTLE EASIER KNOWING EVERYTHING IS TEMPORARY

Do you lock yourself into certain thoughts, feelings, and perceptions, as if everything is going to last forever? Do you tell yourself, "This will never change," or "It's always going to be this way"?

Things will change. And it isn't always going to be this way. Everything—every mood, every experience, every situation—is temporary. Pain is temporary. Fear is temporary. Even grief is temporary—at least the acute pain of recent loss. And it's not just the uncomfortable things. Joy is temporary too. So savor it.

Nothing is permanent. Try living with this belief and you may find you are far more patient, accepting, and teachable. You might breathe a little easier.

Everything is transitory. And it's all there to teach you. So value the moment. It will change in a hurry.

Time is God's way of keeping everything from happening at once.
—Author unknown

DAY 242
TURN YOUR DREAM INTO A PLAN

We talk about our dreams all the time. We muse about things we want to do, see, and be. But how many of us turn our "wouldn't it be nice ifs" into actual plans?

Your dreams have value. They emanate from your core. They are honest, heartfelt, and innocent. But dreams alone won't get you far.

A dream alone is a fantasy…a nice idea…a warm fuzzy. A dream alone is young and idealistic. It's the daydream of the child—beautiful, yes, but over time a source of discontent if it isn't realized.

Don't let your dream remain a dream. Look it straight in the eye, break it down, and operationalize it. Write it out, brainstorm about it, and let yourself be creative, free from judgment and naysaying. Develop goals, action steps, and deadlines. Get practical about turning your dream into a plan.

Honor and act upon your dream, whether or not it becomes a reality in the way you imagined. Just let it flow. Don't let doubt and fear of failure stand in your way.

Your dream is an expression of who you are. Your plan is your road map. Make a habit of turning dreams into plans.

Let yourself be silently drawn by the stronger pull of what you really love.
—Rumi

DAY 243
STAND IN YOUR TRUTH

Are you one of those people who chooses peace in the moment over peace in the long term? Do you find it easier to keep others comfortable than risk the discomfort of speaking up?

Appeasing others in order to keep the peace only hurts us in the end. Our acquiescence is often more about fear than it is about unselfishness and generosity. And it chips away at self-respect.

At the same time, we don't generally keep doing what we are doing unless there are some payoffs. By kowtowing, we get to avoid discord and discomfort. In denying what we want and need—in going along to get along—we never have to stand on our own two feet and take responsibility for ourselves.

In the long run, however, we pay quite a price for our shortsightedness. We give our power away, deny our truth, and water ourselves down.

Stop purchasing peace at the expense of yourself.

He who trims himself to suit everyone will soon whittle himself away.
—Raymond Hull

DAY 244
REMEMBER THE WHY

In business circles, they talk of staying connected to the *why*.

A successful business maintains its connection with its primary motivation—the why behind its work. It preserves integrity by holding on to a sense of mission, knowing its value isn't simply the measure of what it does, but more importantly, why it does it.

This principle isn't limited to the professional arena. Each of us would be well served by identifying and preserving a sense of passion and purpose in this life. We all need to be clear about the *why* so we don't get caught up in the *what*.

Life won't always keep you comfortable. You won't always like your present circumstances. But if you stay connected to your own personal why—to your values, principles and priorities—you will find the significance in it all. You will remain purposeful and focused.

The meaning of life is found in the why. Stay connected to it. Stay connected to you.

Begin each day as if it were on purpose.
—Author unknown

DAY 245
OPEN YOUR HEART

Painful themes from past relationships can put us into hypervigilant, overprotective mode. We try to shelter ourselves from future pain. It's understandable why we would do so.

All too often, however, the guard we put up backfires, isolating us and blocking human connections. What begins as an attempt at self-protection becomes a kind of bondage. We stay in defensive mode long past the presence of pain.

The person who wounded us, for example, may no longer be in our lives, yet we remain closed and suspicious. Guardedness has become a way of life. It's what we know. It's familiar.

Life can't be lived behind walls. Open your heart again. Trust that you can and will take care of yourself with others.

Opening back up takes work, but the payoffs are well worth it.

You can close your eyes to the things you do not want to see,
but you cannot close your heart to the things you do not want to feel.
—Author unknown

DAY 246
LOOK FEAR IN THE FACE

Fear lies to us and distorts our perspective. When we look into the future through a lens of fear, we predict the negative. We anticipate worst-case scenarios. We picture ourselves alone and helpless and overwhelmed.

Fear lies to us about what's to come. It blinds us to all the times we have walked through fear and survived. It blinds us to how much we have grown by facing fear head on.

Many things you once feared you have already walked through. So don't forget how strong you are and how far you have come. Don't overlook all your past and present accomplishments. Don't tell yourself you are helpless to help yourself. You are not.

Whatever happens, you will bring yourself to the situation as you have done so many times before. You will face the fear and grow. And you will be okay.

You gain strength, courage, and confidence by every experience in which you really stop to look fear in the face. You are able to say to yourself, "I've lived through this horror. I can take the next thing that comes along."
—Eleanor Roosevelt

DAY 247
LET GROWTH BE YOUR MOTIVATOR

We tend to look for external motivators to get us going and keep us going. What we often don't recognize is that growth can be our motivator.

Get motivated by being the best *you* that you can be. Every day, in every way, see what you're capable of, and get excited about it. Challenge yourself to think positively, to open your mind, to be proactive about self-care, to allow yourself to dream, to maximize your interactions with others, and to fully show up in your life.

If you can't come up with a specific goal, don't worry. If you don't have a role model to motivate you, fear not. Focus on growth, and let your own evolution inspire you.

Know that as you do so, a wonderful life will take shape.

Waste no more time talking about great souls
and how they should be. Become one yourself!
—Marcus Aurelius

DAY 248
JUST WAIT. IT WILL PASS.

Just as the Universe is ever-changing, our lives are ever-changing. Everything is in a constant state of flux. This truth can be quite liberating.

It enables you to release the tight grip you might have on your here and now. It allows you to let go and let things be. It frees you up to accept and embrace what is and to get the most out of whatever it is you're experiencing, knowing it won't last forever.

Everything passes. This includes the good and the bad, the joy and the pain. There's no need to cling to any of it. You don't have to cling to joy, fearing it may not come again. You need not inadvertently cling to pain, thinking it's going to last forever.

Your present is not a permanent condition. Clinging to anything and calling it permanent only gets us in trouble. We feel disappointment when the joy passes. We fear the pain never will.

Everything is transitory, so let yourself fully experience the moment. It may not come again.

Everything changes; nothing remains without change.
—Buddha

DAY 249
GET DECISIVE

Do you get paralyzed by the prospect of decision-making? Do you worry so much about making the right decision that you make no decision at all? Are you the proverbial deer in the headlights?

Personal freedom hinges on decision-making. It centers on breaking out, breaking free, and being willing to be true to ourselves. It's about letting go of the need to please and being courageous enough to make choices that come from our core. It's being willing to stand by these choices.

Fear not—you can always change course. Nothing has to be forever. It's more than okay to change your mind. Just do something, knowing that doing nothing only keeps you in a holding pattern. It chips away at your sense of self.

Decisiveness, like personal empowerment, is a muscle that needs to be developed. Our decisions shape who we are.

Go ahead. Make a decision. It gets easier.

A wise man makes his own decisions;
an ignorant man follows the public opinion.
—Chinese proverb

DAY 250
GIVE YOURSELF PERMISSION

Many of us hesitate to claim our space in this world, to stand up for ourselves, to ask for our wants and needs, and to do things just for us. We are afraid to seem self-serving or, worse yet, to be inconvenient to others. So we play small. We shrink, lest we put others out.

But there is nothing honorable about playing small. There is nothing noble about self-neglect. You owe it to yourself to take care of *you*. Self-parenting is your right and your responsibility.

Don't worry so much about putting others out that you end up neglecting *you*. Doing for you is not doing to another.

You can look at self-care in one of two ways: You can see it as selfish, which will only keep you playing small. Or you can see it as doing the one job you absolutely must do—being the best parent to yourself that you can be. There are two sides to this coin.

So how will you look at self-care?

> *There came a time when the risk to remain tight in the bud was more painful than the risk it took to blossom.*
> —Anais Nin

DAY 251
EMBRACE STABILITY

Stability is yours for the taking—no matter what.

No matter your situation, no matter how unstable your circumstances, and no matter how unpredictable or chaotic life may seem, stability is yours if you want it. Stability is not the measure of external circumstances; it's an internal state.

Internal stability hinges on healthy self-esteem and personal boundaries. With self-esteem, we honor and respect ourselves. We embrace our inherent worth and value. We know who we are, and we love ourselves no matter what.

With healthy boundaries, we protect and contain ourselves and our internal realities. We decide what we take in and what we don't. We decide how much of ourselves we give away and how much we won't. We know and preserve who we are.

Stability comes from within. It's entirely up to you.

Nothing can bring you peace but yourself.
—Ralph Waldo Emerson

DAY 252
DARE TO BE REMARKABLE

Many of us live in fear of our individuality. We hide ourselves, deny our truth, and fight against who we are. Maybe early on we conformed. We told ourselves we had to. But is this what we should be telling ourselves today?

Think about the messages you craved early on. They were likely the same messages we all wanted to hear: *Be yourself. Live your own life. Be true to who you are.*

Give yourself today what you've always wanted. If you have been disallowing your individuality because you felt it was disallowed early on, it's time to stop.

Embrace your uniqueness. Dare to be remarkable. Get a kick out of who you are.

A wonderful realization will be the day you realize that you are unique in all the world. The world is an incredible unfulfilled tapestry, and only you can fulfill that tiny space that is yours.
—Leo Buscaglia

DAY 253
CHOOSE YOUR FAMILY

You might think that the family into which you were born is the only family you will ever have, but this is not true. You can have another family as well—a family of your own choosing.

It's natural to hunger for close family relations. We are hard-wired to want to be—even expect to be—close with our families of origin. But these expectations, however reasonable they may be, can get us in trouble. When unmet, they can be the source of our own emotional stuck-ness. We find ourselves caught in pain and resentment.

As adults, we have the power to come to our own assistance by healing lingering hurts and disappointments. If our families of origin have let us down, we can create new families. We can surround ourselves today with what we hungered for then. Our friends become our chosen families.

As a child, you didn't get to choose your family. As an adult, you do. And it's never too late to widen your family circle.

Call it a clan, call it a network, call it a tribe, call it a family.
Whatever you call it, whoever you are, you need one.
—Jane Howard

DAY 254
BREATHE INTO THE HOLE WITHIN

Feel like you have a hole inside? A void you try to deny, fill up, or medicate? Do your attempts at evasion and gratification feel temporary because the hole is still there?

Many of us have a hole within. We feel incomplete, insufficient, and unfulfilled. We tell ourselves we are not good enough. We feel subpar. And we try to compensate for it.

We want to pretend the hole isn't there, but it's hard to ignore. So we seek esteem from the outside. We people please. We busy ourselves. We overeat, drink, and drug. And we continue feeling empty.

What if you breathed into that hole instead?

Rather than ignoring or superficially satisfying it, fill it with the one thing you really need. Fill it with the only thing that truly satisfies—self-love.

Put your future in good hands—your own.
—Author unknown

DAY 255
ASSUME POSITIVE INTENT

We do ourselves a profound disservice by assuming the negative, always attributing to others the most harmful of intentions. But many of us do precisely that. Ever on the lookout for wrongdoing, we live in a state of cynical anticipation.

People will disappoint us. It's unavoidable. They will do us wrong, often with the distinct intention of doing so. But why buy trouble by assuming negative intent? Why hold yourself in a perpetual state of distrust?

Anticipating the worst is no way to go. Not only do you keep yourself in chronic angst and misery, you are less apt to recognize positive intentions when they do exist. Since you are unlikely to see the good when it's right in front of you, your negative conception of humankind will only get further reinforced.

Do yourself a favor: if you're going to assume anything, assume the positive. You will know soon enough if your faith is unwarranted.

For beautiful eyes, look for the good in others;
for beautiful lips, speak only words of kindness;
and for poise, walk with the knowledge that you are never alone.
—Audrey Hepburn

DAY 256
EXHALE

Many of us live zipped-up lives.

The experience has been described in all sorts of ways. Some say it's like holding our breath. Some say it's a feeling of containment and constriction. Some have referred to it as living in a suit of armor—one in which we keep ourselves secure and protected.

The bottom line is that we tuck our stuff inside, fearful about showing our true selves and being seen for who we are. We reveal selected, edited parts of ourselves, showing only what we think is acceptable and presentable. In doing so, we deny ourselves intimacy and authentic connections. We deny ourselves our full potential. We deny our humanity.

Freedom is found in unzipping yourself. It's found in unpacking everything you have kept inside and letting it be revealed. There's no need to hold your breath any longer.

Exhale and let yourself be.

No man for any considerable period can wear one face to himself
and another to the multitude, without finally getting
bewildered as to which may be the true.
—Nathaniel Hawthorne

DAY 257
STAND UP FOR YOUR RIGHTS

The Bill of Rights plays an essential role in law and government. A series of limitations on the power of government, it's a powerful symbol of our freedom and culture. It proclaims our natural, unalienable rights as a people.

But how often do we think about our personal rights?

Maybe it's time to identify the privileges you hold dear. Whether you have been living by them or not, outline your basic liberties. Dig deep and think about what you choose to claim.

Create your Personal Bill of Rights and post it somewhere prominent. "As a person I have a right to…." Come up with as many as you can, and get excited about each one. Let them empower and inspire.

Claim your personal rights. Get deliberate about it.

Be gentle with yourself. You are a child of the universe,
no less than the trees and the stars; you have a right to be here.
—Max Ehrmann

DAY 258
BE REAL ABOUT WHO YOU ARE

We try to be people we are not. We pretend, not only for others but for ourselves. We adopt certain characteristics and call them who we are. We become whatever it is we tell ourselves we should be. We then wonder why our lives don't feel like a fit.

Being real can be uncomfortable, but it's the only way to go. The alternative is a life half lived. It's a life of superficiality and pseudo-relationships. It's feeling like an imposter, as if someone else is living your life. Playing to the audience just isn't worth it.

Watch out for saying you're one thing or another when in reality you're anything but. Be real about who you are. Be honest about what makes you *you*. Your life won't feel like your own until you do.

Be careful who you pretend to be. Your life will reflect it.

Honesty is the first chapter of the book of wisdom.
—Thomas Jefferson

DAY 259
OWN YOUR LIFE

Your life won't change until you change your life.

Many of us wait for life to change. We sit in passive observation of our own lives, hoping the tide will shift, wanting things to be different. But we don't take responsibility for making this happen.

If this sounds familiar to you, now is your wake-up call. Pull yourself out of that state of suspended animation. Stop telling yourself you are simply a victim of circumstance, helpless to affect your own destiny. Take the bull by the horns and create a life you can feel good about.

If you keep doing what you've always done, you will keep getting what you've always gotten. So remember, you are in the driver's seat. You are in control of your life experience. You are your own change agent.

Start making some shifts today. Just do something different, re-membering no change is insignificant. Down the road, you will see that one change at a time your whole life trajectory has shifted.

Do you want to know who you are? Don't ask.
Act! Action will delineate and define you.
—Thomas Jefferson

DAY 260
LET PAIN TEACH YOU

Trying to dodge pain and skirt discomfort doesn't work. Pain simply won't be ignored.

We can deny it for a time. We can wall ourselves off from it. But invariably it finds us. What's more, as we exert all sorts of energy trying to circumvent pain, we miss out on something powerful. We miss out on what there is to gain from our pain.

The solution to pain isn't finding a cure for it. The solution to pain is learning and growing from it.

Pain is a gift. It's there to enrich you, make you a better person, and provide you with wisdom and insight. It helps you grow and enriches your journey.

Pain is never wasted if you let it teach you.

We must embrace pain and burn it as fuel for our journey.
—Kenji Miyazawa

DAY 261
KEEP ASKING HOW THINGS COULD BE BETTER

It's important to appreciate today. It's also important to strive for tomorrow.

Believing that things can always be better drives us to show up proactively, to make the most of every day, to maximize opportunities, and to always look for the growth. We celebrate the now while knowing there's more ahead. It's a balance we strike.

Be curious. Stay hungry. Stretch yourself to go beyond the limits of what *is* to what can *be*. Plug into today, and keep your eyes on tomorrow.

There is always room for improvement.

There is far more opportunity than there is ability.
—Thomas A. Edison

DAY 262
GIVE YOURSELF THIRTY DAYS

We often talk ourselves out of personal growth. We feel so daunted by the prospect of change that we end up doing nothing.

Start a thirty-day challenge. It's a great antidote to procrastination and overwhelm. You can do just about anything for thirty days. At the end of thirty days you can reevaluate.

Maybe you will choose to give something up—television, cigarettes, coffee, junk food…even negativity. Perhaps you will commit to a daily exercise regimen. You might choose to journal, read something inspirational, or meditate daily. Maybe you'll work on your attitude by doing affirmations or writing down a few things for which you're grateful each day.

After thirty days you will be closer to a new life habit. You will have experienced the fruits of positive change. You will feel good about yourself for keeping your promise to yourself. Whether or not you keep up the change, the thirty-day challenge is a powerful growth tool.

Start your challenge today.

Ninety-nine percent of all failures come from
people who have a habit of making excuses.
—George Washington Carver

DAY 263
FREE YOURSELF EMOTIONALLY

Children tend to be emotionally free. They express what they feel, and they do so readily. When they are sad, we know it. When they feel joy, they show it. When they are frustrated, they wear it on their sleeve.

However, as we age we often become inhibited. We go emotionally underground as we learn to deny, deflect, and cover up our emotions. We begin labeling our feelings as good or bad and censor ourselves accordingly. We seem to become less liberated and less authentic as we go.

Free yourself. Release your emotions. You will become more yourself as you do.

You can hold back from suffering of the world; you have free permission to do so, and it is in accordance with your nature, but perhaps this very holding back is the one suffering you could have avoided.
—Franz Kafka

DAY 264
REMEMBER, THERE'S ALWAYS A POINT!

Many of us have a "what's the point?" attitude about speaking up. We wonder, "If I can't make a big wave, what's the point in making any wave at all?" There is always a point.

The value of speaking up is not found in outcomes. The value is found in the act of speaking up itself. It's about sharing who you are. It's about being self-revealed. It's about self-advocacy and truth. It's about personal power.

There's a starfish story that speaks to this.

Taking his morning walk on the beach, a man sees thousands of starfish washed ashore. The tide is going out, and the starfish are stranded. He then sees a child bending down, picking up something, and throwing it into the ocean. As he gets close, he sees the child is picking up starfish, one by one, and tossing them back into the ocean.

The man says to the boy, "There are so many starfish on the beach. You can't possibly make a difference."

The boy says nothing at first, then bends down, picks up another starfish, and throws it back into the ocean. "It made a difference to that one," he says.

Stand up, show up, and have a voice. There's always a point.

Stand upright, speak thy thoughts, declare the truth thou hast, that all may share; Be bold, proclaim it everywhere: They only live who dare.
—Voltaire

DAY 265
CHOOSE YOUR PERSPECTIVE

The lens through which we look at life is shaped by our beliefs about ourselves. If we want to change our perspective—and in turn, our overall life experience—we need to choose new thoughts.

If we tell ourselves we are worthy, valuable, and lovable, we will find confirmation of this all around. If we believe we are capable, we will recognize our successes. If we think we deserve, we will allow ourselves to receive. If we believe our wants and needs will be met, we will see clearly the ways they are being met.

If you're not experiencing life as you'd like to, it could be that your perspective is to blame. Change your thoughts and you will change your perspective.

Change your perspective and everything will change.

People who look through keyholes are apt to
get the idea that most things are keyhole shaped.
—Author unknown

DAY 266
WORK FOR YOUR DREAMS

Many of us have some pretty clear dreams and distinct wants. They have been a part of us—a part of our consciousness—for as long as we can remember. But over time, we have become discouraged. "Why wouldn't we be discouraged?" we tell ourselves. Our dreams don't seem to be coming true. But are we working at them?

Maybe it's not that some Higher Power is dangling a carrot in front of us, only to keep our dreams just out of reach in the long run. Maybe we simply aren't doing the footwork to make our dreams happen.

If you have a dream, respect it. It comes from an authentic place within. It's real. It's a part of you. But don't expect your dream to take shape on its own. You will need to co-participate with your Higher Power in making it a reality. You'll have to work at it.

You have the power to make your dreams come true. And when you do the footwork, anything's possible.

Every great dream begins with a dreamer. Always remember,
you have within you the strength, the patience, and the
passion to reach for the stars to change the world.
—Harriet Tubman

DAY 267
PROTECT YOUR POSITIVITY

Your perspective is yours and yours alone, and you get to shape it as you choose. Just be sure you maintain it.

Maximize the time you spend with those who energize. Set limits with those who wear you out. Protect and preserve your positive energy, knowing negativity drains and positivity sustains.

When you feel depleted, bring yourself back. When you've let your perspective be co-opted, get centered again. Take charge of your reality. Get rejuvenated. Recommit yourself to peace and positivity.

Choose your outlook, care for it, and keep the positive energy flowing. Don't let anyone rain on your parade.

A positive attitude may not solve all your problems,
but it will annoy enough people to make it worth the effort.
—Herm Albright

DAY 268
BE RELIGIOUS ABOUT SOMETHING

This isn't about religion. This is about dedication and commitment. It's about choosing to do something that's good for you. It's about discipline, initiative, and perseverance. It's an inner drive to which you faithfully respond.

Being religious about something helps you reach your goals. It enables you to feel good about yourself. It earns you respect from yourself and others. It gives you a measure of success and satisfaction.

Being religious about nothing keeps you from your goals. It erodes self-respect. Without direction and dedication, you never get to see what you are capable of if only you had applied yourself—if only you had believed you were worth it.

Promise yourself you will get religious about something. Big or small, it doesn't matter. What matters is your stick-to-itiveness—the building block of self-respect. This is what shows you what you're made of.

Get dedicated. Create a discipline and keep it up. It won't take long to feel the results.

No life ever grows great until it is focused, dedicated, and disciplined.
—Harry Emerson Fosdick

DAY 269
BACK THE TRUCK UP

Do you tend to get ahead of yourself, pushing yourself too hard, too fast? Do you crank up anxiety by doing so?

Watch out for driving yourself so hard that you never stop to acknowledge what you think, feel, want, and need. By staying one step ahead of where you are, you lose touch with your core. You arrest your own healthy development. You become a stranger to yourself.

Don't let this happen. And if it is happening, take a breather and check in with yourself. Carve out some time and space to get grounded again. Turn back toward yourself.

Sometimes you just have to back the truck up and catch your breath.

Nature does not hurry, yet everything is accomplished.
—Lao Tzu

DAY 270
OWN YOURSELF

On our journey to personal freedom, we reclaim what we have disowned along the way. We love again the self we have neglected. We embrace the parts of ourselves from which we have been running.

Wounding doesn't heal when we try to escape it. It heals when we move toward it and walk through it. Otherwise, it will continue to own us. We can disguise our wounding, but it's there. We can reject aspects of ourselves that got injured along the way—parts we think are unseemly—but they won't be ignored in the long run.

Embrace who you are. Embrace all of you.

The next time you feel angry, judgmental, resistant, anxious, needy, or depressed, try learning from whatever it is that's triggering you, instead of shutting down to it. You just might find something you have been denying or disowning. You just might find a wounded self in need of some tenderness.

Welcome that wounded you with love and truth. Parent it, love it, and heal it. Reconnect with the person you've been neglecting.

You deserve to be whole again.

Don't forget to love yourself.
—Soren Kierkegaard

DAY 271
WAKE UP

Does it feel like life is happening to you? Like you are a victim of present circumstance, a pawn in the game of life, powerless to effect change? You could be signing up for your own pain.

We often put ourselves in harm's way. We go to the places where we are likely to get hurt. We let others cross our boundaries. We cling to unrealistic expectations. We do the same things over and over, expecting different results. It's as if there's a contract for pain, and we keep signing on the dotted line.

We do it because we think we don't deserve better. We do it because we got wounded along the way and life has lied to us about our worth and value. We do it because our boundaries are weak. We do it because we have grown accustomed to pain. It has become habitiual to put ourselves in a victim postition. It's what we know.

It's time to wake up to how you've taken over where history left off. It's time to take responsibility for how you experience life. You are the architect of your reality.

We can let circumstances rule us,
or we can take charge and rule our lives from within.
—Earl Nightingale

DAY 272
RESPECT YOUR PAIN

Often we compare our pain to others' pain. We judge it. We critique it. We wonder if we have a right to feel it.

But pain is pain. We all have it. In our own ways, in our unique circumstances, we all hurt sometimes. To measure our pain by deeming it significant or insignificant, worthy or unworthy, is to deny the very real experience of it. It denies others' experiences of pain as well.

What if you let go of all the judgment and comparison? What if you stopped analyzing and just accepted? What if you took responsibility for your pain?

Respect your pain and you will learn from it. Lean into it and you will work through it like never before.

Your pain is the breaking of the shell that encloses your understanding.
—Khalil Gibran

DAY 273
MAKE YOUR LIFE A REFLECTION OF YOU

Take a close look at your life. In fact, study a typical week in the life of *you*. Does it accurately reflect who you are? Is it congruent with your authentic self?

Incongruence is being one person inside and another on the outside. It's misalignment between who you are and how you live. It is passion unfulfilled and hunger unsatisfied. The emotional experience ranges from deep pain to apathy. Either way, it's never good.

Peek in at your life and see if it looks like you. If it doesn't, things have to change. Design life as a tribute to what makes you uniquely you. Respect yourself enough to do so.

Make your life a perfect reflection of who you are and what you love.

And in the end, it's not the years in your
life that count. It's the life in your years.
—Abraham Lincoln

DAY 274
LET THE LIGHT IN

Personal freedom hinges on being able to find opportunities in brokenness. We embrace vulnerability and learn from it, making the most of the times when our exteriors crack. It is in these moments we are revealed. It is in these moments we grow.

As hard as we try, life won't let us stay shrouded by defenses and coping mechanisms. We all get exposed sometimes. The question is how we respond. Will we zip ourselves up, hold it together, and keep up appearances? Or will we embrace our humanness, honor and release our feelings, and allow ourselves to be vulnerable and real?

You are not meant to survive life. You are not meant to be impervious to pain. You are meant to be human, to feel your feelings, to be fully revealed at times, and to grow from it all.

Whatever it is that causes a chink in your armor, it's a moment of truth. Lean into the vulnerability and learn from your brokenness. Then you can let the light in.

Celebrate the cracks. And if it's too much to celebrate them, make the most of them.

> *Ring the bells that still can ring*
> *Forget your perfect offering*
> *There is a crack in everything*
> *That's how the light gets in.*
> —Leonard Cohen

DAY 275
KEEP GROWING AND CLARITY WILL COME

We wait and wait, hoping clarity will come knocking. We get stuck in our own analysis paralysis, locking ourselves in perpetual contemplation, fooling ourselves into thinking if we deliberate hard enough and long enough the answers will come. It doesn't work this way.

We grow our way to clarity. We grow our way to the outcomes we seek and to the futures for which we yearn. We bring about conclusions by doing something, not by sitting, frozen in suspended animation, contemplating our navels.

If you feel stuck, do something. If you want clarity, take action. If you want a life you can feel good about, it's time to get moving.

You have to do your own growing
no matter how tall your grandfather was.
—Abraham Lincoln

DAY 276
GIVE YOURSELF NOW
WHAT YOU DIDN'T GET THEN

We grew up in imperfect settings. We were raised by imperfect people. Mistakes were made. But we don't have to keep tripping over what we didn't get early on. If we do, we may continue feeling victimized, disempowered, resentful, and bitter.

We don't have the power to make right what was wrong then. But we do have the power to do things differently from today forward, and in so doing, to heal the past.

What was it that you wanted and needed? Was it love, acceptance, or validation? Was it patience, forgiveness, or understanding? Was it peace, serenity, and the absence of chaos?

You have more power over your past than you may think—not in rewriting history, but in giving yourself today what you didn't get then. If you hungered for love and acceptance, love and accept yourself. If you yearned for forgiveness, forgive yourself. If you wanted peace, carve out peace for yourself. Be both the healer and the healed.

Eliminating the pain of the past is possible. Why not begin today?

I have always been delighted at the prospect of a new day,
a fresh try, one more start, with perhaps a bit of magic
waiting somewhere behind the morning.
—J. B. Priestley

DAY 277
FREE YOURSELF FROM SELF-JUDGMENT

Judgment is inherently toxic. Whether it's our own self-judgment or judgment from others, it diminishes us. It stifles spontaneity and freedom. Over time, it becomes embedded in our own belief system, woven into how we relate to ourselves and others.

Negative judgment is clearly damaging. It disempowers and weakens. It puts our worth and value up for debate, causing us to question ourselves. We live in fear of this negative judgment. We live in fear of our unworthiness.

Positive judgment can be toxic as well, though it hurts less and is wrapped in a prettier package. It's still about measurement and comparison. It puts us in an approval-seeking posture in life. We chase validation. We live in pursuit of acceptance.

Get off the judgment roller coaster altogether. Stop depending on the positive. Stop living in fear of the negative.

Live and let live.

If you judge people, you have no time to love them.
—Mother Teresa

DAY 278
EXPECT SOME DISCOMFORT

As humans, we seek pleasure and shy away from discomfort. We want life to be easy. We want it to be smooth and seamless. When it isn't, we make up all sorts of unhelpful theories.

We tell ourselves we shouldn't have to struggle so much. We wonder why we do. Maybe we are inherently unlucky. Maybe we were born under some kind of black cloud, and that's why we get all the bad breaks. Whatever we tell ourselves, we have bought into the myth that life is meant to keep us comfortable.

Life isn't meant to keep you comfortable. Life is meant to challenge you. And it's your responsibility to learn from life's challenges, knowing that growth is made up of many uncomfortable moments. Pleasure is temporary, but the gifts of discomfort can be rich and lasting. Try to be grateful for the bumps instead of always trying to dodge them.

Life is bumpy. Expect it to be. Now lean into the discomfort.

Learning is not child's play; we cannot learn without pain.
—Aristotle

DAY 279
DECIDE TO BE HAPPY

Happiness is a decision. And deciding to be happy is about taking action. It's about choosing to come to our own assistance. It's about making the changes in our lives that will bring us greater contentment. It's a concrete process with concrete steps.

Think about what makes you happy and go do it. Engage in activities that bring your life meaning. Make choices from your gut. Practice gratitude. Foster spirituality. Nurture your relationships. Let go of emotional obstacles to happiness, such as resentment and unforgivingness. Get proactive about getting happy.

You were born with precisely what you need to be happy. You were born with the potential to make choices that foster your own joy. You are capable of creating a life you love.

You are capable of happiness.

People are just as happy as they make up their minds to be.
—Abraham Lincoln

DAY 280
START FRESH

Have you been perpetrating against yourself the same negativity you experienced early on in life? Have you been blaming, shaming, judging, and limiting yourself? If you didn't like it then, why are you doing it now?

It's not a choice we make. It's sheer habit. We take over where our histories left off, treating ourselves the way we were treated. We might be deliberate about some of our choices, consciously doing certain things differently, but when it comes to our relationships with ourselves, we tend to do what we know to do—until we learn better.

Create some new traditions. Be good to yourself. Treat yourself the way you always wanted to be treated. It will take work, but you can do it.

Any day is a good day to start fresh.

What we call the beginning is often the end. And to make an end is to make a beginning. The end is where we start from.
—T. S. Eliot

DAY 281
CHOOSE YOUR THOUGHTS CAREFULLY

You've likely heard about the law of attraction in recent years.

When you approach life with a good attitude and a healthy belief system, you feel positive. When you feel positive, you show up confidently and proactively. When you show up confidently and proactively, you create positive experiences. The Universe rearranges itself according to your beliefs.

As simplistic as this theory may sound, there's truth to it. We generate and magnify what we believe. We construct our own experience. We notice, gravitate toward, and create more of whatever matches our fundamental beliefs. If we have an optimistic outlook, the Universe feels supportive to us.

As you experience positive things and create abundance, your optimistic outlook strengthens. You see the Universe as a friendly and plentiful place, conspiring for your good. The Universe confirms your belief system. It's a positive feedback loop.

Opt for an optimistic attitude. Your life will reflect it.

You create your own universe as you go along.
—Winston Churchill

DAY 282
KNOW THAT WITH EACH TEAR YOU CRY, YOU'RE HEALING

As I was grieving a profound loss in my life, someone said to me, "Just remember, you will never have to cry this same tear again." When I thought about what he had said, I was struck by its profoundness. Of all the clichés, of all the sayings and suggestions that were being tossed my way, this one stood out. This is the one that stuck with me. I share it with clients to this day.

"You will never have to cry this same tear again." In other words, our tears are directional. Our tears have purpose. No tear is for nothing, and no tear is ever wasted. By letting ourselves cry our tears, we are letting ourselves heal. Each tear is clearing us out for something new. Each tear is moving us through our pain.

When you find yourself in the throes of pain—when the tears just want to come—be sure to allow them. You are getting somewhere. You are moving yourself along, even though it might feel as if you're standing still. And just remember, you'll never have to cry this same tear again.

To weep is to make less the depth of grief.
—William Shakespeare

DAY 283
DO THE THINGS THAT MAKE YOU HAPPY

What makes you happy? What gives you that lighthearted feeling? What do you love so much that you lose yourself in it?

This may sound like a pretty obvious suggestion: do the things that make you happy. But many of us do anything but.

Don't judge what makes you happy. Just acknowledge, honor, and celebrate whatever it is that puts a smile on your face. Then ask yourself if you are engaging your passions and pursuing what you love.

Many of us know what makes us happy. We can rattle off our list of passions with enthusiasm. But if asked to look at the amount of time and effort we actually devote to these, it wouldn't be much. Awareness isn't enough. Action matters.

Don't delay. Go out and do the things that bring you joy. And when you feel the happiness that comes from deliberately following your bliss, make sure you pause, take a breath, and savor the experience.

Even if happiness forgets you a little bit,
never completely forget about it.
—Jacques Prévert

DAY 284
MAKE THE MOST OF THE MOMENT

It's easy to get overwhelmed by the prospect of change. We look ahead to where we want to be and feel daunted by how we will ever get there. We tell ourselves that the growth we need is just too intimidating to undertake.

All change begins in an instant. It begins with a new awareness, a personal insight, or one of those eye-opening *ahas*. It starts the moment something clicks.

Try not to be discouraged by the task at hand or by the amount of time you think it will take to live the life you want. Don't get ahead of yourself. Your new life will be shaped one moment at a time.

Don't miss the moment that's right in front of you. It only takes an instant to wake up.

All glory comes from daring to begin.
—Eugene F. Ware

DAY 285
START LIVING NOW

We often delay our own happiness without knowing it. We postpone it in our hunger for perfection. We wait for things to be just right before we give ourselves permission to be happy. In doing so, we keep happiness out of reach.

It seems we are caught in an illusion—the illusion that life can and will ever feel just right. But life isn't perfect. It never will be. Being human is untidy and unpredictable.

Don't wait for things to be perfect before you start living. Don't put off your happiness any longer by making it contingent on some fantasy of perfection. Don't let yourself get caught in that trap.

Claim happiness today. Do it right in the midst of all that messiness and imperfection.

Happiness is a journey, not a destination; happiness is to be found along the way, not at the end of the road, for then the journey is over and it's too late. The time for happiness is today, not tomorrow.
—Paul H. Dunn

DAY 286
BE A CHARACTER

You are distinctive. You are special. There is only one of you. But do you allow yourself to stand out?

Character is the sum of one's unique traits and distinguishing qualities. It's inherent and enduring. It's inimitable.

Each of us is a character—a true individual. Yet many of us play ourselves down, change our shape, and settle for being a type or a persona instead.

Freedom is expressing who you are and celebrating the character that is you. So go ahead—be a character!

I want freedom for the full expression of my personality.
—Mahatma Gandhi

DAY 287
PERSIST

Each of us is talented. Each of us has gifts and passions. But what are we doing about them? And what do we do when talent isn't enough?

What matters is not what makes you unique. What matters is how you use everything that makes you unique. It's putting your talents into practice. There is nothing so maddening and discouraging as having passions you're not actualizing, endowments you're not honoring, and gifts you're not sharing.

Talent isn't enough. If you want to create a life you love, identify and hone all that makes you *you*. Grow your passions. Engage your delight.

Be relentless about it.

Persistent people begin their success where others end in failure.
—Edward Eggleston

DAY 288
LOOK FOR THE COUNTERBALANCE

At times of suffering it feels like everything is out of balance and out of whack. It seems there is so much bad and not nearly enough good. Life appears arbitrarily cruel and unfair.

On the other side of bad, however, there is good. On the other side of ugliness there is beauty. On the other side of grief there is healing. And on the other side of pain there is peace. Things are not as unbalanced as they seem.

For everything there is a counterbalance—a divine gift that awaits us on the other side of suffering. In the moment, our distress outweighs everything else. But in the big picture, there is another side to the coin. There always is.

Look for it and you will find the counterbalance, maybe not today, but one day. Watch as that divine balancing act plays out yet again. Watch as hope is again restored.

Although the world is full of suffering,
it is full also of the overcoming of it.
—Helen Keller

DAY 289
LET YOURSELF BE AFRAID

We reject fear. We mask it. We ignore it. We medicate it. We try to busy our way past it. We do anything and everything not to feel fear.

It seems we have bought into the great lie about fear. We see it as weakness. We think being strong means never being afraid. Because of this perception, we dance around fear, desperately attempting to bypass it. We think we have to.

We all get scared. It's natural. What isn't natural is denying this, rejecting our humanness, and ending up controlled by fear. What we deny comes to own us eventually.

You don't have to fear *fear* any longer. Embrace it, lean into it, and move through it. Allow it to instruct you. Let it show you where your hunger is—your hunger for growth and expansion. Walk through the fear to the gifts on the other side.

It's okay to be afraid. It's okay to be nervous, especially about change and growth. It usually means that what you fear is important to you.

Whatever it is you're wanting, you won't achieve it by dodging your fear.

Don't be afraid to see what you see.
—Ronald Reagan

DAY 290
KEEP MOVING

None of us evolves through intention alone. We don't grow and change by contemplating our next move yet doing nothing about it. We need to take action.

To develop self-esteem, we need to be proactive. We need stick-to-itiveness. We have to remind ourselves regularly of our inherent worth and value. We need to engage in esteem-able acts. We need to practice the art of loving ourselves.

Changing our belief system—another central part of our journey to personal freedom—requires more than desire. We identify negative thinking, create positive reframes, repeat them regularly, and live our healthier thoughts by showing up in alignment with these. With practice, our new thoughts transform into new core beliefs.

Creating a life you love requires that you move proactively toward self-knowledge and authenticity, getting to know yourself more all the time. It calls you to create goals and act on them, not simply identify them and leave them on a shelf somewhere. Passivity won't do.

If you want change, do something.

Always keep moving toward your goals. We keep moving forward,
opening new doors, and doing new things, because we're curious…
and curiosity keeps leading us down new paths.
—Walt Disney

DAY 291
GIVE YOURSELF UNEXPECTED LUXURIES

Many of us have grown accustomed to feeling badly about ourselves. We have gotten used to less than good enough. We are familiar with playing small. We expect we will keep feeling more of the same.

If you've adapted yourself to this painful status quo, then concepts such as self-esteem and self-acceptance seem like luxuries. Don't let this stop you from pursuing them. Don't tell yourself you don't deserve such things.

Give yourself unexpected luxuries. For some, self-esteem and self-acceptance are basic concepts. For many, they are pure extravagance.

Don't shy away from the unforeseen. Embrace the novelty of self-love. Pamper yourself. You deserve it.

I don't like myself, I'm crazy about myself.
—Mae West

DAY 292
FREE YOURSELF FROM THE SHOULDS

Should is often a shame-laden word. Yet for many of us, it's absolutely habitual. It has become woven into our life script.

Sure, there are times when should is appropriate. There are things we should and shouldn't do in this life. Shoulds can keep us on track. But they can also get away from us. They can permeate our life experience. They can be a sign of something wounded within.

We *should* ourselves for our thoughts, feelings, behaviors, choices… even our very being. We restrict our freedom with all sorts of rules about what we should think, feel, and do. We keep ourselves down by shaking that self-condemning bony finger in our own direction.

If you wonder which shoulds are healthy and which are toxic, notice how you feel. When you say them, do you feel encouraged or discouraged, empowered or disempowered? The way you feel says it all. Shame is an unmistakable experience.

Perhaps it's time to stop shoulding yourself; if you want your personal freedom, you're going to have to.

Everyone needs a sense of shame, but no one needs to feel ashamed.
—Frederick Nietzsche

DAY 293
DECIDE WHAT KIND OF PERSON YOU WILL BE

Have you allowed life circumstance to define you? Has your sense of self been co-opted by everyone but you? Do you feel lost and undefined? And have you been contributing less than your best because of it?

They say more harm in this world comes from people who have never made a decision about who they are and how they want to be. Conversely, more good has been done, more love has been shown, and more kindnesses has been expressed by people who made a conscious decision to be good.

It's time to self-define. It's time to choose who you are and who you are going to be. It's time to make a decision. Your life is the sum total of your choices.

Decide who you are. If you don't, life will decide for you.

Between stimulus and response there is a space.
In that space is our power to choose our response.
In our response lies our growth and our freedom.
—Viktor E. Frankl

DAY 294
REVEAL YOURSELF

The masks we wear keep us isolated and alone. They disconnect us from the human family. They block genuine relations with others. They keep our wants, needs, and dreams out of reach.

You likely began disguising yourself in order to feel worthy, valuable, and accepted. You probably now know that it doesn't work. Because the path you follow isn't your own, you don't feel fulfilled by it. You feel as if you're on the outside looking in at your life.

Stop disguising yourself. Take off the masks you've been wearing. Break out of the illusion that you need to be anyone other than who you are.

You are a unique creation. The world deserves you. You deserve you.

In every man there is something which to a certain degree prevents him from becoming perfectly transparent to himself, and this may be the case in so high a degree, he may be so inexplicably woven into relationships of life which extend far beyond himself that he almost cannot reveal himself. But he who cannot reveal himself cannot love, and he who cannot love is the most unhappy man of all.
—Soren Kierkegaard

DAY 295
CLAIM POWER WHERE YOU HAVE IT

There is freedom in claiming power where we have it. It's empowering to change what we can, rather than frustrate ourselves focusing on what we can't.

There are bound to be areas of your life in which you feel powerless. It's unavoidable. But you can't let this helpless feeling contaminate the rest of your life. Like a drop of food coloring in a glass of water, a feeling of powerlessness can color your whole life experience if you allow it to.

Take stock of where you have power, and put that power into action. Take charge of your life anywhere and everywhere you can.

If you're going to color your life, color it with empowerment.

You may never know what results come of your action,
but if you do nothing there will be no result.
—Mahatma Gandhi

DAY 296
BUFFER YOURSELF

Do you feel like a sponge? You start off your day dry and airy, but by day's end you're heavy, saturated, and filled to capacity? Do you feel like you have to wring yourself out, only to get soaked all over again?

If life seems to burden and deplete you, and if you want to remedy this, boundaries are the name of the game. Boundaries are healthy personal limits that protect and contain your inner reality. They preserve your sense of self. They keep you from becoming so weighed down by life that you lose yourself in the mix.

Each of us gets bombarded by information throughout the day. We need to be discerning about what we do and do not take in. We need to determine what is ours and what belongs to others. We need to identify where we do and do not have power, reminding ourselves where we end and other people begin. We need to self-preserve.

Don't be a sponge. Be something far less permeable.

Not everything that can be counted counts,
and not everything that counts can be counted.
—Albert Einstein

DAY 297
BE A FRIEND TO YOURSELF

Maybe you have heard the saying, "If I had a friend who talked to me the way I talk to myself, I would have kicked them to the curb long ago!"

Are you your own worst critic? Are you tougher on yourself than anyone else is or ever has been on you? Have you been tolerating the intolerable?

If so, stop. Become your own best friend and supporter. You know your strengths, passions, weaknesses, and vulnerabilities. You can be a friend to yourself like no one else can.

Clean up that adversarial relationship with self. With friends like that, who needs enemies?

Love yourself, accept yourself, forgive yourself,
and be good to yourself, because without you the rest
of us are without a source of many wonderful things.
—Leo F. Buscaglia

DAY 298
WALK THROUGH THE DOOR

It's pretty natural to want to escape pain, to try to dodge the distress of difficult times, and to skip the experience if the experience is uncomfortable.

But life is our teacher. And to skip the experience is to skip the lesson. To choose not to feel our feelings is to miss out on the gifts on the other side of them—gifts like strength, healing, humility, empowerment, and endurance.

We invite into tomorrow what we don't process today. Avoiding all the hurts, unresolved wounds, pain of past losses, frustrations, and disappointments causes them to simply linger—and fester. They become functionally autonomous within us, taking on lives of their own.

In our attempt to circumvent discomfort, we end up clinging to the emotions we have been trying to avoid. We prolong the experience from which we have been running.

Look your emotions straight in the eye instead. Own them. Metabolize them. And persevere.

Whatever it is, walk right through it.

The way out is through the door.
Why is it that no one will use this method?
—Confucius

DAY 299
STAY CHECKED IN

I will always remember the diver's watch.

It was big and bulky and something she always wore. On the hour, every hour, that watch would beep. No matter what she was doing it would go off. When it did, she would close her eyes for a moment, be still, and continue whatever it was she was doing.

I always wondered what it was all about. Was there some profound significance to the clock striking the hour? Had something important happened on the hour at some point in her life? Had she simply set the alarm once and never figured out how to clear it?

Finally I said something. "Mind my asking what the diver's watch is all about?" She paused for a moment. "You know," she said, "I've been so completely disconnected from myself for so long, that if I only check in with myself once every hour, I figure that's pretty darn good!"

Wow. That diver's watch was a reminder to check in with herself. It was about deliberately going within and asking herself how she was doing. It was about staying connected with her core. What a concept.

Find a way to check in with yourself. See what you're thinking, feeling, wanting, and needing. Maintain conscious contact with *you*.

A diver's watch will surely do.

When your heart speaks, take good notes.
—Judith Campbell

DAY 300
RING YOUR OWN BELL

Don't depend on others to turn you on and get you going. Motivate yourself.

To rely on forces outside of you to activate your life force is unreliable and unpredictable. The world won't always buoy and sustain you. It's never wise to hitch yourself to anyone else for direction.

Other people do inspire us. They wake up certain sleeping tendencies within us, and this is a wonderful thing. But banking on external sustenance is risky. We end up feeling empty and ineffective when we fail to achieve someone else's dream for us.

Your own encouragement is what counts. You are the authority on *you*, so be your own change agent.

Ring your own bell.

A man who finds no satisfaction in himself seeks it in vain elsewhere.
—Francois de la Rochefoucauld

DAY 301
CREATE A MENTAL MOTTO

What motivates and ignites you? What keeps you enthused? Can you think of a catch phrase that captures this? This can be your mental motto.

A mental motto is a guiding principle—an internal inspiration. It's a mantra or slogan. It's short yet potent. It directs you and keeps you on track. It holds you accountable. It summarizes where you are and sets the tone for where you want to be.

A mental motto sounds something like: "I'm a student of life." "Life is to be lived." "I am the change I want to see in the world." "Don't worry; be happy."

Another chapter in life might call for a different motto. Just capture your prevailing perspective at the time, knowing that living in accordance with it will build confidence and satisfaction. There's power in setting an intention and living by it.

Have fun creating your personal motto. Then live your life by it. Let it inspire you to become more of who you are and who you've always been.

If I have the belief that I can do it, I shall surely acquire the capacity to do it even if I may not have it at the beginning.
—Mahatma Gandhi

DAY 302
GET DELIBERATE ABOUT GRATITUDE

Today I am grateful for _____.

Fill in the blank. It's a good habit to get into. Every day things happen for which we can be grateful. Why not identify, document, and celebrate them?

Think about starting a gratitude journal. Jot down three things for which you're grateful each day. The practice will cultivate a grateful heart. You will come to magnify the positive in life. You will feel good about keeping this daily commitment to yourself. What's more, as you reflect on your entries, you will learn about yourself and what you love.

There are other ways to be intentional about gratitude. You could send a gratitude letter. You could keep a gratitude journal for someone you love. You could begin a gratitude practice with your mate, making a habit of sharing gratitude with each other each day or keeping track of gratitude throughout the year. You could give gratitude gifts on birthdays and other special occasions. However you do it, get deliberate about being grateful. And start now.

Today I am grateful for _____.

What did you come up with?

God gave you a gift of 86,400 seconds today.
Have you used one to say "thank you"?
—William A. Ward

DAY 303
LET YOURSELF MAKE U-TURNS

Do you allow yourself to change course? Or do you lock yourself in to decisions, even when it's clear things aren't working out as you planned?

Changing course sure gets a bad rap. We can be called fickle, flakey, or incapable of sticking with a plan. But what's so terrible about changing our minds?

Very often the healthiest thing you can do is make a U-turn. You learn from what isn't working, and you make adjustments. Always open and teachable, you grow wiser with life experience. You are humble and willing to try again.

Don't hesitate to turn yourself around. It's more than okay to change your mind.

The important thing is this: to be ready at any moment
to sacrifice what you are for what you could become.
—Charles Dickens

DAY 304
GET PASSIONATE

Do you feel excited about life? Do you have an inner enthusiasm and drive? If not, it's time to find your passion.

See what lights you up throughout the day. Don't judge it; just notice it. A blue sky, a smile from a friend, some yummy food, a creative endeavor, a satisfying work experience…whatever it is, pay attention. If you can't find passion in your daily activities, reflect on what you think would ignite you. What do you daydream about?

What you're looking for is your passion—your life force and spirit. Fully engaging this is how you achieve great things in your life—great on your own personal scale. Living passionately is about living a life of meaning.

Find that passion. If you're struggling to find it, keep looking. It will turn up.

Nothing great in the world has been accomplished without passion.
—Georg Wilhelm Friedrich Hegel

DAY 305
GIVE YOURSELF A BANNER DAY

We want things to go right. We want to be successful. When our heads hit our pillows at the end of the day, we want to know everything went well. We want that banner day.

What makes a banner day? For many of us, it's a day when things go well by some outside standards—a day when people, circumstances, or the fates keep us comfortable. Maybe we see it as a day when we are recognized by others, when we garner external esteem, and when we are on and it pays off.

To label a day successful simply because your world keeps you comfortable, however, is to give circumstances far too much power over you. There's another way to look at this, and it doesn't rely on externals, nor does it rely on windfalls, praise, or performance.

Don't wait for the world to keep you comfortable. Don't wait for the stars to be perfectly aligned in order to be happy. Don't tell yourself you have to perform a certain way in order to count your day a success. Just show up and be who you are. Be the same person inside as you are on the outside. Be successful by being authentic.

Give yourself a banner day every day.

Most folks are about as happy as they make up their minds to be.
—Abraham Lincoln

DAY 306
LET YOUR INSIDE DEFINE YOUR OUTSIDE

We often let the outside define the inside. But it needs to be the other way around.

Basing our internal state on our external circumstance is dangerous business. Our sense of self, our serenity, and our stability will be here one minute and gone the next, all depending on what's occurring around us. It's not the way it's meant to be.

Choose your perspective and you choose how you experience your world. By claiming authority over your internal reality, you can find stability and serenity in situations where you previously felt none. It's all about what you bring to the table.

Foster positivity within and you will engage in your world from that place. You will feel satisfied by your circumstances since you are interpreting your life with a healthier perspective. You will shape positive outcomes because you approach things with positive motivation. Your life will mirror back the spirit with which you approach it.

A positive feedback loop will develop between your inner and outer worlds. You will find yourself in healthy conversation with your circumstances.

You will design a life you can feel good about.

The last of the human freedoms is to choose your
attitude in any given set of circumstances.
—Victor Frankl

DAY 307
EXTERNALIZE THE LITTLE YOU

When you can't seem to figure out how to come to your own assistance, when you don't know how to comfort and care for yourself, and when you need to pull yourself out of the darkness but you're not sure how, there is an answer.

Picture a little child. This little being is separate from you, perhaps right in front of you. It might be you as a young child. It might be the idea of a little child. Either way, imagine what he or she is thinking and feeling. Then let your loving instincts determine your actions.

What does this child need when feeling helpless and scared? In times of pain and sadness? What does this child need to feel safe, secure, and comforted? To feel loved and nurtured? Motivated and supported? Let your heart give you the answers. Let the parent within you step forward.

A loving reminder, an affirmation or validation, a few words of encouragement, a comforting activity, a peaceful break...maybe just a little something yummy to eat or drink. Whatever it takes, do it for *you*. This is the essence of self-parenting.

The answers are within you.

Think what a better world it would be if we all—the whole world—had
cookies and milk about three o'clock every afternoon and then
lay down with our blankies for a nap.
—Robert Fulghum

DAY 308
DECIDE WHAT KIND OF WORLD YOU LIVE IN

Our perceptions shape our entire reality. The way we look at life determines how we experience it. Our outlook is the product of core beliefs—some we chose, some were handed to us—and it either works for us or against us.

What kind of universe do you live in? If you see it as an unfriendly one, your perspective is likely hurting you, and it's time to make a change. Decide how you want to see your world and in turn, how you experience life.

Choosing a positive perspective will give you a sense of comfort and serenity. It will motivate and inspire you. It will enable you to scan for the good.

So what kind of world do you live in? It's your choice. It's a critical one.

The most important decision we ever make is whether we believe we live in a friendly universe or a hostile universe.
—Albert Einstein

DAY 309
BUILD THAT MUSCLE MEMORY

Creating any new skill is a deliberate process. It takes time and repetition. Developing new emotional, mental, and spiritual capacities is no different.

Self-esteem, healthy personal boundaries, the ability to self-advocate, and other life skills require commitment and practice. They might feel unnatural at first, but with time and dedication they become familiar. They become our new normal.

Learning to ride a bike or drive a car was a deliberate process. We had to think carefully about every step. In the same way, as we do the work of our personal freedom, we have to be highly deliberate and focused—until we don't have to be anymore. As with riding a bike or driving a car, we create muscle memory. We reach a point where it all feels natural.

Don't give up just because it feels difficult, stilted, and strange. Persevere. The muscle memory will come.

Patience and perseverance have a magical effect
before which difficulties disappear and obstacles vanish.
—John Quincy Adams

DAY 310
BE TRUE TO YOUR YESES AND YOUR NOS

No is such a simple little word. Why do we avoid it?

There was a time we could say no. As kids, we said it with conviction. We said it with power. We said it with pride. No was our first exposure to boundaries. No was a line we drew in the sand. It was our personal limit.

Over time, however, many of us became people pleasers, and no got dropped from our vocabulary. We replaced it with indecision, self-doubt, and the need to keep others comfortable at our own expense.

We became *yes* people. We told ourselves we didn't have a right to our own lives, to our autonomy, to our limits. We said yes because we didn't allow ourselves to say no. When we did muster a no, we qualified it with explanation and justification.

But no is essential. No protects you. No tells you where you end and others begin. Being strong enough to say no means you can genuinely say yes.

Make your yeses and nos count. Make sure they come from an honest place within. They speak volumes about who you are.

Half of the troubles of this life can be traced to
saying yes too quickly and not saying no soon enough.
—Josh Billings

DAY 311
BE A GREAT PARENT TO YOU

Some find the concept of self-parenting a bit hokey. But it's actually a very practical concept. We need to take responsibility for ourselves. We need to take charge of our own development.

What makes a great parent?

Most would agree a healthy parent is present, available, and accepting. A healthy parent embraces a child's humanness, forgives and teaches a child to forgive, and loves unconditionally. A healthy parent celebrates uniqueness, rejoices in accomplishments, and encourages a child to dream big. A healthy parent teaches personal responsibility and accountability, while remaining humble and teachable, always striving to be better.

Doesn't it make sense that by giving ourselves these same gifts we would thrive? Just as the developing child blossoms in such an environment?

Now it's your turn. Today you take over being the healthiest parent you can be—to *you*.

You, yourself, as much as anybody in the
entire universe, deserve your love and affection.
—Buddha

DAY 312
BELIEVE IT NOW

It's natural to want to know the future and be able to count on it. We want not only to believe good things are possible; we want to know what those things will be. We think we need this in order to be inspired and motivated.

Even though it's impossible to know the future, we buy into the misconception that we need to see clearly all the good that's possible in order to show up today in faith. We ask ourselves, "If I can't picture it, how can I believe in it?"

It's a matter of trust. It's choosing to believe. It's letting go of the need to script everything ahead of time.

Tell yourself there is good to come, that change is possible, and that your best possible future will be shaped by plugging into life, in faith, one day at a time.

You've been living the old way a long while, and it's hard to picture what change will look like. Just believe it's possible, and jump into the journey.

A new and wonderful life is awaiting you if you choose to believe.

Some things have to be believed to be seen.
—Ralph Hodgson

DAY 313
STAY CURIOUS

Are you asking enough questions?

One of the most powerful tools for feeling alive and actively engaged in life is curiosity. It keeps us alert, receptive, and hungry for life experience, eager to know and learn more.

Curiosity keeps your mind active. It opens up new worlds. It brings excitement to life.

Be inquisitive. Sink your teeth into life. There is so much to learn, so stay open.

Be a lover of newness.

Wherever we are, what we hear is mostly noise.
When we ignore it, it disturbs us.
When we listen to it, we find it fascinating.
—John Cage

DAY 314
RUN ON A FULL TANK

Are you an intensity junkie? Do you push the limits because doing so makes you feel purposeful and alive? Do you keep going and going, even when you know it's time to refuel? Are you running on empty?

Intensity and busyness can be a reaction to our histories—a learned way of coping. We dodge our emotions through doing. Over time, we become so disconnected from ourselves that we keep pushing and pushing without noticing it's time to stop and catch our breath.

Running on empty doesn't work. You will lose yourself in the process. It's okay to take a break and refuel.

Those fumes will only get you so far.

Happiness is not a matter of intensity but of
balance and order and rhythm and harmony.
—Thomas Merton

DAY 315
PLAY THE ADULT

We wouldn't stay stuck in victim mode if there weren't some payoffs.

By being a victim, we get attention. We get coddled and cared for. We escape responsibility and risk-taking. We get to feel powerful by feeling right. We avoid growing up.

As good as the payoffs might be, the victim position is anything but powerful. In being a victim, you relinquish control over your life. You shut yourself off from your own power. You tell yourself the world is against you, and you feel alone in that one-down mindset. You remain an emotional child.

Being adult is better than you think. To be adult is to be in charge of your life and your destiny. It's to be self-determined and self-defined. It's to be answerable to *you* and you alone. To be adult is to be free.

Break out of the victim mentality, take responsibility for yourself, and choose to grow up. Then you can become who you were always meant to be.

We grow neither better nor worse as we get old, but more like ourselves.
—May Lamberton Becker

DAY 316
LOOK FORWARD

"It's so much easier to stay in recovery than it is to get into recovery." This is something I've been saying to clients in addiction recovery for years. I actually believe it applies to everyone.

If you've got some momentum going, don't stop now. If you're moving forward, keep it up. Try to do one thing every day to nurture and grow yourself.

Leaving behind the forces that have held you back takes practice and drive. And it's much easier to stay on the path than it is to get back on it. So do what you promised you would do. Honor your commitment to yourself. Work on your personal growth each and every day. It doesn't have to be anything too substantial; just do something.

Whatever you do, don't turn back. Keep looking forward.

Even if you are on the right track, you'll get run over if you just sit there.
—Will Rogers

DAY 317
LET YOUR LIGHT SHINE

Whatever lights you up, whatever sets you on fire, it's yours and yours alone—and you have a right to it. You deserve your enthusiasm. It's your birthright, and you get to claim it.

No more hiding your light under a bushel. No more playing yourself down and subduing your own passion. There is nothing enlightened about diminishing who you are.

Devote your time to what you love. Let the world see you. Allow your talents to be revealed and your dreams to come alive. Don't be sheepish about it.

Get enthusiastic. Take a lively interest in life. Shine brightly!

Let us endeavor to live so that when we come
to die even the undertaker will be sorry.
—Mark Twain

DAY 318
KEEP YOUR FORK

Do you know the story about the woman and the fork?

A woman had been given a short time to live. She was talking with her pastor, picking out songs for her service, choosing the outfit in which she would be buried, and finalizing other details.

When everything appeared to be in order, she remembered one thing she had forgotten to mention to her pastor: she wanted to be buried with a fork in her right hand. The pastor, understandably puzzled, asked her to explain.

She said she always loved how, at the end of special meals as plates were being cleared, she was told, "Keep your fork." It meant something wonderful was coming. She loved hearing those words.

She knew that those who viewed her in her casket would be wondering why the fork was in her hand. She wanted the pastor to be sure to explain. She was keeping her fork because "the best is yet to come."

Live in a spirit of good things ahead. Hold on to positive expectancy. The best is yet to come.

Our faith in the present dies out long before our faith in the future.
—Ruth Benedict

DAY 319
GO AHEAD, FORGIVE YOURSELF

Self-forgiveness is an act of self-acceptance. It means we understand we are imperfect—that we are human beings who have faults and make mistakes. We love ourselves in the face of our humanity, when we are at the bottom and the top, when we are keeping ourselves comfortable and when we are not.

Many of us worry that self-forgiveness is somehow selfish and self-serving. We withhold it because we think it's unjustified. We opt for guilt and shame instead. We think they're somehow noble.

Choosing to embrace our humanness and imperfection—to take responsibility for ourselves as well as forgive—is enlightenment. This frees us to show up compassionately with others. In reality, guilt and shame are the more self-serving paths.

Forgiving ourselves isn't easy. It takes effort to let go of what's old and familiar. Do it anyway.

It will be well worth it.

Forgiveness does not change the past, but it does enlarge the future.
—Les Brown

DAY 320
GET A PROJECT

There is power in a project. Working on and toward something gives us a sense of purpose. It motivates and inspires. It keeps us going and keeps us growing. It gives us a reason to get up in the morning.

Is there something you've been meaning to explore but haven't committed the time? Do you have a running list of ideas and interests, none of which you've pursued with any consistency and dedication? Have you been shortchanging yourself by not sticking with things?

Dust off one of those long-neglected aspirations and take action. If you don't have a project waiting in the wings, find one. Pursue it with passion and diligence.

Get a project and dedicate yourself to the task. It speaks volumes about your commitment to *you.*

I am only one, but still I am one. I cannot do everything,
but still I can do something; and because I cannot do everything,
I will not refuse to do the something that I can do.
—Edward Everett Hale

DAY 321
LIVE A BIG FAT LIFE!

Every child comes into this world with inherent spontaneity and openness. All one has to do is watch a child at play to see that natural exuberance and freedom in action. But if we were spontaneous and open as children, why aren't we as adults? What happened along the way to suppress that spirit?

What happened was that we learned to play small. We learned to self-limit. We learned to suppress our dreams and stay under the radar. We learned not to claim our space in this world.

If you learned to play small—if you have gradually quieted yourself over the years—it's likely due to things that happened to you or limitations that were imposed on you. It's all about what you learned and how you were treated. Today you get to give yourself a do-over.

Today you can treat yourself differently. Today you can relate to yourself in a whole new way. You have just as much power to release those limitations as others had to impose them.

Break free from beliefs that drag you down and limit your life force. Burst out of self-restriction. No more playing small in order to get by.

Live BIG instead.

You see things; and you say, "Why?"
But I dream things that never were; and I say, "Why not?"
—George Bernard Shaw

DAY 322
DECIDE WHAT YOU'RE GOING TO FEEL

Believe it or not, you have a say in what you feel.

Feelings are not random. Feelings are more than arbitrary emotional energies that come over us, rendering us powerless in their presence. Much of the time, they are more an effect than a cause.

To a large extent, our thoughts drive our emotions. It is what we tell ourselves that creates an emotional response. Choose the thought and we choose the feeling. Change the thought and we can change the feeling.

You have so much more power over your emotions than they have over you. So what do *you* want to feel?

When we direct our thoughts properly, we can control our emotions.
—W. Clement Stone

DAY 323
MODERATE YOURSELF

Moderation is the key to a happy existence. As distasteful as this may sound, it's true.

Living life in extremes, in an all-or-nothing mentality, is intense. And intensity, while it might feel exciting and alive, isn't healthy. It's erratic and unpredictable. Being on one minute, off the next, high one minute, low the next, full on then full off, is no way to live.

Freedom is the ability to respond to life rather than react to it. Freedom is about balance, peace, and healthy personal limits. It's living an even-keeled kind of existence, as unappealing as this may sound to those intensity junkies out there.

If you must be immoderate, be immoderate with good feelings. Be immoderate with positivity and exuberance.

Just watch out for the other stuff.

Moderation is the center wherein all philosophies,
both human and divine, meet.
—Benjamin Disraeli

DAY 324
BE FREE WHEREVER YOU ARE

True personal freedom is not contingent on anything external. Rather, it's an internal experience. It's a state of being.

Personal freedom is self-acceptance. It's liberation from limitation, lingering wounding, and restrictive thinking. It's the absence of resistance. It's autonomy and self-determination. It's being unapologetic about who we are.

When you are free within, you are free always. Wherever you are, you are free. Whatever situation you find yourself in, you are free.

Personal freedom is yours for the taking.

Emancipate yourselves from mental slavery;
none but ourselves can free our mind.
—Bob Marley

DAY 325
BE UNAPOLOGETIC ABOUT WHO YOU ARE

Living unapologetically means we allow ourselves to be fully authentic. We live from our core, completely congruently, the same inside as we are out. We walk in alignment with our true self, ever connected with our sense of inherent worth and value. We embrace our natural spontaneity and openness. We are liberated. We are real.

This doesn't come easily to all of us. Being authentic may feel anything but natural.

People may try to get you to conform to their way of thinking. They may judge you and try to shame you. They may react with envy and resentment.

Stay the course. Be strong. Be who you are. Surround yourself with your best supporters.

You deserve an unapologetic life. You deserve to be unabashedly you. Any guilt you feel about it was learned along the way, and you can unlearn it.

You have within you what it takes to become the full expression of who you are.

Hard times arouse an instinctive desire for authenticity.
—Coco Chanel

DAY 326
DECIDE WHAT FREEDOM MEANS TO YOU

We all love freedom, and we all want it. But what exactly is it?

Is it the right to choose? Is it the power to think for oneself? Is it inner peace and tranquility?

Think about what freedom means to you, and define it for yourself. Reflect on your life's journey, including past struggles, limitations, and obstacles. Notice what has been lacking. Observe your hunger. Consider the hope and vision you have for your future.

Decide what freedom means to you. Then go after it with vengeance.

Freedom is the oxygen of the soul.
—Moshe Dayan

DAY 327
WATCH FOR REPEAT PERFORMANCES

Our personal freedom depends on self-knowledge, insight, and the ability to look within so as to avoid repeat performances—those familiar but often unhealthy patterns of living and reacting. We know them well, but they're clearly not working for us.

To experience life anew we have to open ourselves to change. Only then can we break the insanity habit—that tendency to do the same things over and over again, expecting different results. We need to believe that a new way is possible—that we don't have to show up as we always have.

Every day you get opportunities to learn about yourself. Every day you get chances to make a shift. When you see yourself doing the same things over and over again, wake up and think about what you could do differently. When you find yourself waiting for things outside of you to change, look at how you can change them.

Repeat performances mean something isn't changing that needs to. Go deeper than habituated behaviors. True transformation happens at the core.

Bad habits are easier to abandon today than tomorrow.
—Yiddish proverb

DAY 328
STAY HUNGRY

There's a hunger deep within us for meaning and purpose. But many of us silence this hunger. We quiet the curiosity within. We sublimate our desires and stunt our own growth. The price we pay is an uninteresting and disenchanted life.

Make friends with that hunger. Listen to it. It will keep you moving, learning, discovering, and dreaming. It's your passion, your purpose, and the source of personal progress.

Be hungry for challenges, opportunities, and change. Be hungry for new experiences and enlightenment. This hunger will propel you forward and help you create a life you love.

If you want a future you can feel good about, stay hungry.

If happiness is the absence of fever, then I will never know happiness. For I am possessed by a fever for knowledge, experience, and creation.
—Anais Nin

DAY 329
PRACTICE AUTHENTICITY

Every day we get to exercise our authenticity. Like any healthy habit we are forming, like any new skill being honed, authenticity takes practice. Many of us have to work at it.

As you move through your day, make choices that are aligned with who you are. Speak up for yourself. Be honest about what you think and feel. Allow yourself to be imperfect. Ask for what you want and need. Practice healthy personal boundaries. Say no when it's sincere to do so. Say yes when yes feels right.

Practicing authenticity is about showing up and plugging in, not as others expect you to, but as you expect *you* to.

Now go out there and be authentic.

The shortest and surest way to live with honor in the world
is to be in reality what we would appear to be.
—Socrates

DAY 330
SING YOUR OWN SONG

For Native Americans, singing is sacred. It's a form of prayer. It's a means of communicating with higher powers. It's a way of passing along cultural customs. It's a part of daily life.

As one Native American educator said, "In our culture, everyone sings." It's a powerful concept. There's much we can learn from it.

Many of us are looking for our own voices. We want to feel valued and accepted. We want our uniqueness to be celebrated. We want to feel like we have something to say.

"Everyone sings" reminds us that we each have a song to sing. We each have something special to say. We each deserve to be heard.

Don't keep the music bottled inside yourself. Sing the song you were meant to sing.

Speak your truth, even if your voice shakes.
—Author unknown

DAY 331
LET YOURSELF BE SEEN

"Pay no attention to the man behind the curtain," warns the Wizard of Oz. He doesn't want anyone to see the real person—the ordinary man behind the veneer. He doesn't want to be exposed as the charlatan he is.

Can you relate? Are you afraid to be who you really are? Do you worry about being found out?

Living life in hiding is a pseudo-existence. It's a painful state of incongruence between inner and outer selves. It's a façade.

Perhaps it's time to come out, show yourself, and dispose of the fear of people paying attention. Maybe it's time to let go of the pretense.

Let people in. Let them see you.

Let the world know you as you are, not as you think you should be,
because sooner or later, if you are posing, you will forget the pose,
and then where are you?
—Fanny Brice

DAY 332
GO AHEAD, UPSET THE APPLE CART

Does fear of putting others out or putting them off cause you to stay silent? Do you deny who you are because you don't want to rock the boat?

It's okay to put people out sometimes. It's okay to rock the boat.

We can't carve out our unique paths in this life without expecting some resistance from others. We can't chart our own courses without stepping on some toes. Our wishes will bump up against others' sometimes. Our choices will rub others the wrong way. Our truth will often disappoint. All of this is inevitable if we are going to be true to ourselves.

On your journey to personal freedom, be prepared to sit in some discomfort. Be willing to displease others at times. Get a little uncomfortable in order to be true to yourself.

Now, this isn't about barreling your way through life willy-nilly, indifferent to your impact on others. It's about standing in your truth and owning your power.

As long as you move through this life with honor and grace, there's nothing wrong with ruffling some feathers.

Be who you are and say what you feel, because those who
mind don't matter, and those who matter don't mind.
—Dr. Seuss

DAY 333
INJECT INSPIRATION INTO EVERY DAY

If you want an inspired life, create an inspiring environment for yourself. Keep yourself motivated. Encourage yourself daily.

Doing so will keep you energized and hopeful. It will help you maintain forward momentum. It will prevent self-sabotage and keep you from throwing in the towel on your dreams.

There are endless ways to inspire yourself. Write a personal mission statement. Create a personal motto. Make a dream board. Start a vision journal. Read about your heroes. Study their successes and document your own. Remind yourself of your assets. Celebrate who you are and how far you've come.

It is you who can best inspire yourself. It is you who can be your greatest supporter.

Inject some inspiration into your day today. Then do it again tomorrow.

Shoot for the moon. Even if you miss, you'll land among the stars.
—Les Brown

DAY 334
SATISFY YOUR HUNGER

There's a certain kind of hunger that drives us to accept just about anything we think will feed us. We seek nourishment for what is lacking inside. We find ways to get fed, but they're temporary and superficial.

Being hungry for a sense of worth and value, for a feeling of belonging and purpose, for anything we missed out on early in life, is risky. This is the hunger we try to feed externally—in people, places, and things, in roles, accomplishments, and performance. We feed ourselves with false gods, yet we seem to remain hungry.

However, when we take responsibility for our hunger—when we commit to finding true satisfaction within ourselves—we lose the need for momentary sustenance. We no longer feel compelled to accept anything and everything to fill us in the short term.

Pay attention to that hunger. Notice the source of it and the futility of past attempts to feed it. Seek true sustenance.

Only you can satisfy this hunger.

You have brains in your head.
You have feet in your shoes.
You can steer yourself in any direction you choose.
You're on your own.
And you know what you know.
You are the guy who'll decide where to go.
—Dr. Seuss

DAY 335
GET BUSY GETTING REAL

Being who we are isn't something we automatically know how to do. Many of us have no idea how to be our true selves.

Perhaps we didn't feel encouraged and supported early on in life. Perhaps we got the message that it wasn't okay to be who we were. Maybe we learned external-esteem rather than self-esteem. We learned to live superficially. We detached from our authenticity. We began playing to the audience rather than living from our core.

If this sounds like you, then you'd best get busy getting real. It will take dedication, purpose, and effort. In fact, it's one of the great paradoxes of our journey to personal freedom: It takes work to get real. It takes effort to become natural. It won't happen on its own.

Get down to the business of being you. Grow into who you've always been.

Become who you are.
—Friedrich Nietzsche

DAY 336
PRACTICE HAPPINESS

Happiness isn't something you are born with or without. It isn't something over which you are powerless. It isn't something you either have or don't have.

Happiness is developed. It's a habit. As with any healthy habit, you have to work at it.

The development of a new habit starts with intention. We determine what we want and why we want it. We then get down to the business of honing certain behaviors until they form our desired habit.

When we slip, we remind ourselves to keep going—the work is well worth it. We remind ourselves that what we want is within our reach. We affirm ourselves and continue practicing. Over time the new habit becomes natural. We create a new normal.

Cultivating happiness requires commitment, dedication, and a willingness to do the required footwork. Devote yourself to this worthwhile pursuit. Be single-minded and persistent.

Happiness is serious business.

Turn your face to the sun and the shadows fall behind you.
—Maori Proverb

DAY 337
DECIDE YOU ARE READY NOW

When we are going through tough times, it's natural to wonder when things will turn around. We hope this is as low as we are going to go. We worry things might even get worse.

It is said that we have to hit bottom—whatever our personal bottom might be—in order to make the changes we need to make. While this might be true, there's an important point to be made: we decide what our bottom is and when we have hit it.

Whatever it is you're struggling with, make up your mind that this is as far as it's going to go. Decide you're ready to change. You don't have to wait and wonder.

Do you want to know if this is your bottom? Just tell yourself it is. Then enjoy the upward journey from there.

The first step towards getting somewhere is to decide
that you are not going to stay where you are.
—Author unknown

DAY 338
CHECK IN WITH YOURSELF

Stop. Breathe. Take a moment to get intentional.

Many of us live lives on autopilot, never pausing to see if we are being true to ourselves. We are so used to agreeing to certain things and disagreeing with others that we have lost sight of who we are.

Create even the smallest stop gap between trigger and reaction and you will begin hearing your own voice. You will begin finding true self.

Before you utter another knee-jerk *yes* or automatic *no*, pause. Before doing anything out of sheer habit again, especially something relevant to your journey to authenticity, catch your breath and see what the real you says.

Your personal freedom demands that you stop, pause, and check in with *you*.

> *Go within every day and find the inner strength*
> *so that the world will not blow your candle out.*
> —Katherine Dunham

DAY 339
CALL THEM THE WONDER YEARS

Everything in your life has brought you to this moment. Everything has shaped who you are. None of it has been for nothing.

If you've embarked upon a journey to personal freedom, embrace it fully. Don't tarnish your enthusiasm by asking, "Why didn't I do this sooner?" "How could I have waited so long?" "What about all the years I wasted?" Just celebrate that you're now on the path—that at last you are awake. The best is ahead.

Just because yesterday didn't look quite as good as today doesn't mean it was for nothing. You were living your life, most likely the best way you knew how. You might have only been surviving, but you were alive. And yesterday brought you to this moment.

Don't call any part of the past wasted. Look at it, learn from it, and start right now to shape a different life for yourself.

> *The best day to plant a tree was twenty years ago.*
> *The second best day is today.*
> —Chinese proverb

DAY 340
BE VICTORIOUS

As adults, no one can take our power unless we give it away. No one can make us feel *less than* without our permission. If we believe we are in charge of our lives, there's no reason to turn that authority over to anyone else.

It's when we don't feel in charge of our own lives that we get into trouble. We let others dictate what we think, feel, and do. We let circumstances control us. We give others sovereignty over ourselves. Then we feel victimized.

How you manage your personal power determines whether you are a victim or victor, whether you are weak or strong, and whether you are other-defined or self-defined. Remember, if you are feeling victimized, you are giving your power away. You are relinquishing your freedom of choice.

Take back your power. Take back power over your experiences, past and present. Take back power over how you interpret your history. Take back power over your thoughts and feelings. Take back power over your freedom.

Say goodbye to that victim mentality once and for all.

The best years of your life are the ones in which you decide your problems are your own. You do not blame them on your mother, the ecology, or the president. You realize that you control your own destiny.
—Albert Ellis

DAY 341
WATCH OUT FOR RABBIT TRAILS

Will the decision in front of you bring you closer to your goals, to your dreams, and to yourself? Or are you headed down a rabbit trail?

Each decision point is an opportunity. It's a chance to move toward our vision and grow our dreams. It's a chance to come closer to self, to become more fully who we are. Even the smallest, most seemingly insignificant decision is an occasion to cultivate authenticity. We need to make the most of these decision points.

Stay the course means we continue forward in spite of obstacles. We pursue our goals no matter what. Don't we owe it to ourselves to do so?

Make sure the moves you make keep you on your chosen path. Stay the course and watch out for getting sidetracked.

Those rabbit trails might be tempting, but they're a waste of precious time and energy.

> *Stay the course, light a star,*
> *Change the world where'er you are.*
> —Richard Le Gallienne

DAY 342
BE A STUDENT OF LIFE

If life is a continuous learning experience, then nothing is ever for nothing. Every experience has value. Every moment is a teachable moment.

It's a wonderful way to approach life—to hunger for self-knowledge, to seek out significance, to choose the healthiest possible perspective no matter the circumstance, and to always grow. It's a life philosophy, one that keeps you conscious and aware, grateful for new opportunities for learning.

The student of life sees nothing as arbitrary or empty. The student of life finds meaning in everything. No experience is ever wasted.

Be teachable. Your life will be richer for it.

We have no friends; we have no enemies; we only have teachers.
—Native American saying

DAY 343
SURROUND YOURSELF WITH POSITIVE PEOPLE

Take a look at the people with whom you surround yourself. Are they positive or negative, encouraging or discouraging, glass half full or glass half empty?

While it's true that no one can make us think or feel anything without our permission, that we are responsible for our internal realities, and that we need to generate positivity from within, it's also true that other people affect us. So we have to wonder, are we buoyed by the people around us or dragged down?

It's asking a lot of ourselves to be impervious to external influences, unaffected by the energy around us and the people in our lives. It takes a lot of energy to fend off negativity so as to preserve inner peace.

Make sure you surround yourself with people who support and enliven you. Take a look around.

It might be time to make some adjustments.

You're not going to make me have a bad day.
If there's oxygen on earth and I'm breathing, it's going to be a good day.
—Cotton Fitzsimmons

DAY 344
KNOW WHAT GETS YOU
OUT OF BED IN THE MORNING

What fires you up and gets you going? What puts a smile on your face just by you knowing you have it ahead of you that day?

Maybe it's being with the person you love romantically. Perhaps it's spending time with your kids. It might be your vocation—or avocation. Maybe it's your art, music, or some other creative passion. Perhaps it's learning, exploring, or being of service to others.

Know what you love, and move in that direction. Give yourself opportunities to engage in the things that bring you happiness. Any day is a good day to get excited about something. That energized feeling isn't just for special occasions.

No more drifting along asleep at the wheel. Know what gets you out of bed in the morning. Embrace the blank slate of a new day.

Rest in reason; move in passion.
—Khalil Gibran

DAY 345
FIND THE GROWTH

Loss can be painful. It can also be the beginning of something wonderful.

Your personal freedom hinges on your ability to pull the good out of pain, to become stronger for every loss, and to find a way to rise up, even when things feel painfully heavy. To free your spirit from the bondage of life circumstances is to be truly free.

Life can be cruel sometimes. Endings are inevitable, but they're only half of the story. Beginnings are the other half.

Remember this and you will find the beauty and growth.

Life doesn't accommodate you; it shatters you. It is meant to,
and it couldn't do it better. Every seed destroys its
container or else there would be no fruition.
—Florida Scott-Maxwell

DAY 346
BE GOOD ENOUGH

It's important to strive for goodness. It's important to be true to your values, to live with integrity, and to do the most you can with who you are. It's important to be the best *you* that you can be.

Make sure, however, that you're appropriately motivated. Make sure you strive for these things because you want to be the healthiest version of yourself possible—the best possible steward of all you are and all you've been given.

Watch out for thinking you have to be good in order to be lovable. Watch out for thinking you need to please and perform in order to deserve. Watch out for telling yourself you have to earn your worth and value. They can't be earned.

Your motivation matters immensely. Instead of working so hard at being worthy, try working at being you. The rest isn't up for debate.

You've been worthy and valuable all along.

What I am is good enough if I would only be it openly.
—Carl Rogers

DAY 347
LET YOURSELF DESERVE

I deserve.

Many of us shy away from this thought. We do so because of a low self-image. We think it's somehow selfish, egotistical, or flat-out unjustified to acknowledge, even to ourselves, that we deserve.

This is not about deserving superficial things like money, acclaim, and good fortune. It's about deserving basic human rights like self-esteem, self-acceptance, and personal freedom. Shrinking back from the concept of "I deserve" speaks volumes about us.

You deserve to feel worthy, valuable, and lovable. You deserve to accept yourself. You deserve to find your own personal freedom. We all do.

So go ahead, say it...

I deserve.

As the day turns into night, keep your worries out of sight. No matter how hard the world may seem, you still deserve the sweetest dream.
—Author unknown

DAY 348
SAVOR EXPERIENCE

No experience is ever wasted. There is something to be learned, gifts to be gained, and riches to be had—in everything.

Seen in this light, everything has a positive angle to it. Everything is an opportunity. It's a chance to become stronger and more enlightened than before. Think of some of the experiences one would typically label bad. Then look at the gifts to be had in each one.

Perhaps you are confronted with a medical crisis. Through this experience you might learn about self-care, about the importance of coming to your own assistance, and about savoring life. Perhaps you experienced trauma in your childhood. In confronting and healing it, you learn about your worth, value, preciousness, and personal rights. You might connect with these in a way you never would have without the call to deliberately rise up from a painful past. Maybe you have lost a loved one and you grow through grief in profound ways. Whatever the challenge, it's a chance to develop yourself.

We all have pain in this life, but it need not be for nothing. When we stay teachable, when we savor life experience as an opportunity for growth, when we hunger for understanding and enlightenment, and when every character in our lives is our teacher, then indeed…

It's all good.

God will not look you over for medals, degrees, or diplomas, but for scars.
—Elbert Hubbard

DAY 349
GO ON A PERSONAL PILGRIMAGE

A pilgrimage is a journey to a sacred place. For the purpose of this reading, that sacred place is your inner self. This is your personal voyage of self-discovery.

Determine where you are headed. If your destination is personal freedom, set your sights on an authentic, liberated self. Get clear on your desire and your vision. Then plan your pilgrimage. Think about how you will get where you want to be.

Take pleasure in the journey. Make it a joyful one. Stay focused on the positive outcomes you seek while embracing the promise of today. Knowing where you're headed, and why, will be pleasurable and gratifying in and of itself.

Each day you will grow further into your true identity. Little by little you will become the person you were born to be.

Start your pilgrimage today.

The greatest explorer on this earth never takes voyages as long as those of the man who descends to the depth of his heart.
—Julien Green

DAY 350
ALLOW

On our way to freedom, we release resistance to abundance and potential. We stop telling ourselves things are impossible. We push through those *I can't* roadblocks.

Resistance is any thought, belief, or behavior, conscious or unconscious, standing in opposition to our desires. What are you holding on to that's keeping you from your dreams? How would life be different if you were freed from that resistance? The stories you tell yourself might be holding you back.

It's amazing what awakens within us when we get out of our own way, when we identify and release those oppressive internal messages, and when we let go of resistance.

If you're not experiencing life as you want to, you have the power to make a change. See what happens when you simply *allow*.

Most of the shadows of this life are
caused by our standing in our own sunshine.
—Ralph Waldo Emerson

DAY 351
DECLARE YOUR INDEPENDENCE

On your journey to personal freedom, you might have some fun creating your own Declaration of Independence. It can be very empowering.

Your personal declaration will likely emphasize some of the same principles as our country's Declaration. We are all equal. Each of us has a right to life, freedom, and happiness. Some may try to take away our basic rights, so we have to speak up and protect them. What else will you add? What else will you declare?

Break away, stand apart, and start living the life you desire. Start living the life you deserve.

Any day can be your Independence Day.

It is not because things are difficult that we do not dare;
it is because we do not dare that they are difficult.
—Seneca

DAY 352
TAKE STOCK

It's important to look in at your life every now and again. It's important to pause and catch your breath. We all need a little perspective sometimes.

A vacation, a weekend away…even a nice long car ride is a chance to pull back from your present experience long enough to more objectively assess it. When you allow yourself to do so, you will see things more clearly. Options will present themselves. Choices will become more obvious.

Step back and get some perspective. Create pauses in your current existence. Take time to take stock.

Your vision will become clear only when you can look into your own heart. Who looks outside, dreams; who looks inside, awakens.
—Carl Jung

DAY 353
CALL YOURSELF BELOVED

You are valuable. You are lovable. You matter. But do *you* believe it?

There is no emptiness like the emptiness of feeling unworthy. If you feel unworthy, you have likely felt this way for a long time. Over time, it has become a self-fulfilling experience.

If we believe we are unworthy and unlovable, then around any corner we can find confirmation of this belief. We read our world through a self-deprecating lens, and we are disappointed by what we find. We become cynical and disillusioned. We feel alone.

Start calling yourself worthy and lovable and your world will confirm it. You will open yourself up to love. You will feel beloved because you are calling yourself beloved.

Reach out. Join life. You are worthy.

If you would be loved, love and be lovable.
—Benjamin Franklin

DAY 354
GET BUSY LIVING

For many of us, it comes down to a simple choice.

It's a choice we face at life's crossroads. It's a choice we also face each day of our lives. We can choose action or inaction, purpose or passivity, growth or stagnation.

Will we move closer to ourselves or farther away? Will we shape lives we love or continue accepting the lives we have been handed?

Stay awake, be proactive, and make a move in the direction of pure freedom.

Get busy living. Do it today. Then by all means, do it again tomorrow!

There is no value in life except what you choose to place upon it,
and no happiness in any place except what you bring to it yourself.
—Henry David Thoreau

DAY 355
BE A TREE

Wouldn't it be wonderful to be strong, stable, and settled into who you are? To have an enduring sense of self, unshaken by circumstance?

Be a tree.

A tree is grounded. A tree has roots. It sways in the wind and bends its branches, but it's fundamentally fixed. It has a sense of permanence about it. It's established and steadfast. You can be too.

Get to know yourself, stand in your truth, believe in your worth and value, and hold firmly to your convictions. Be that tree, so rooted in who you are that the world can't possibly make you doubt yourself.

No more being blown over by the wind. No more being unsettled and ungrounded.

It's time to grow some roots.

Nothing profits more than self-esteem,
grounded on what is just and right.
—John Milton

DAY 356
NOTICE MIRACLES

We tend to see miracles as these one-in-a-million occurrences—extraordinary, mystical events afforded only a select few. We wish miracles would happen to us, but because of how we define them, they don't.

Miracles are happening all the time. Acts of kindness and generosity, moments of forgiveness and mercy, happy surprises and unexpected blessings, shifts in attitude and perception, even the simplest moments of beauty and love—these are all miracles. And they abound.

Whether or not you've known it, you live in a world of miracles, and a healthy sense of wonder and amazement is yours for the taking.

Miracles are around every corner. You just have to notice them.

Miracles are natural. When they do not occur something has gone wrong.
—Author unknown

DAY 357
FIND YOUR INNER GENIUS

Each of us has a unique inner genius. The key is bringing this genius to the surface.

Do some soul searching. Discover who you are and what you're good at. Be honest with yourself, reflect on what ignites you, and celebrate what makes you *you*.

There are countless ways to feel energized and enthused, countless ways to make a difference, and countless ways to be a bright light.

We are all geniuses in our own ways. Find your inner genius and you'll find yourself.

Today you are You, that is truer than true.
There is no one alive who is Youer than You.
—Dr. Seuss

DAY 358
KEEP LEARNING

Whatever you do, never stop learning.

It's something my grandfather used to say all the time. He knew full well that learning is the key to thriving. It's the secret to feeling fully alive. It endows us with a sense of purpose, freshness, and excitement in this life.

Watch out for a been-there-done-that attitude. Beware of giving yourself the message, however subtly, that your growth days are behind you, that you've learned all you can lean, and that there's not much more to discover.

Life is about possibility. It's about perpetual change. There is so much yet to learn and endless ways to learn it. So open your mind. Be receptive. Always seek to improve and understand yourself and your world. Be a seeker and a lifelong learner.

Your questions are more important than your answers. Keep asking them.

Get over the idea that only children should spend their time in study. Be a student so long as you still have something to learn, and this will mean all your life.
—Henry L. Doherty

DAY 359
REMEMBER SELF

It only takes an instant to wake up.

However the disconnect you're experiencing came about, it's time to reconnect. It's time to lean into, rather than away from, who you are. It's time to get real.

Over time, many of us have lost ourselves. Little by little, day by day, we have slipped away, disconnecting from our core. Self-abandonment has become a chronic condition.

But you can remember yourself at any time. When you do, things will at last become clear. Your path will begin to be illuminated. You will find answers where you thought there were none. You will start feeling empowered, awake, and alive.

Nothing is worth pulling us away from ourselves, causing us to self-abandon. Thankfully, it only takes an instant to remember self.

The moment is now.

Do not squander time, for that is the stuff life is made of.
—Benjamin Franklin

DAY 360
SAVOR GROWTH

The day will come when you surprise yourself. The day will come when you say something, in a certain way, as you never would have said it before. The day will come when you realize how far you've come.

These are sweet moments. These are the moments when your personal growth shows itself, when all the work you've been doing comes to fruition, and when the functional you rises up—without even intending to.

Let's say you've struggled with personal boundaries. You've had difficulty standing up for yourself and asserting your limits. You've been working to improve this. Then the day comes when you overhear yourself setting a crystal clear boundary. "That doesn't work for me." "I'd prefer you not do that." "NO."

"Who said that?" you wonder, only to find it was you. It seems healthy responses have become natural. It seems you've created a new normal.

Savor these moments. With perseverance they will keep on coming.

You can do anything you decide to do. You can act to change and control your life; and the procedure, the process, is its own reward.
—Amelia Earhart

DAY 361
EXPECT SOME OVERLAP BETWEEN OLD AND NEW

Life is a series of overlapping stages. As we usher in the new, we gradually phase out the old. It is a transitional process.

Slowly and steadily, we evolve into new and improved versions of ourselves. We know the old thoughts, feelings, and behaviors will linger a while. We also know they'll phase themselves out in time.

Think about a tide moving in and out. Notice how it pushes forward, then pulls back a bit, then surges ahead even farther. Our personal development is much the same.

The old self pulls us backward here and there. It resists growth and change. But we press on with ever-deeper conviction. We don't let ourselves become discouraged by the presence of the old. We know what matters is the general progression.

Be patient with yourself. Expect overlap between the old and the new. Keep your eyes on the tide.

Have patience with all things, but chiefly have patience with yourself.
Do not lose courage in considering your own imperfections but instantly
set about remedying them—every day begin the task anew.
—Saint Francis de Sales

DAY 362
MAINTAIN AMAZEMENT

You deserve a sense of wonder in this life. It isn't just for some; it's for all. Reach out and grab it, because it's yours for the taking.

Start looking for the magic in life. Marvel at all that's wonderful. Embrace new experiences. Seek growth continually. Get excited about what you discover.

To live in a state of amazement is to feel alive, awake, aware, and in awe of the gifts of this life. It's a sense of curiosity, hope, and enthusiasm, a feeling of lightness and youthfulness. It's the ability to look for the good. And when you look for it, you will always find it.

Amazement awaits you around every corner. The world is a wondrous place—as long as you decide that it is.

There are only two ways to live your life. One is as though nothing is a miracle. The other is as though everything is a miracle.
—Author unknown

DAY 363
DECIDE ABOUT YOUR FUTURE

Personal freedom is achieved one moment at a time. With every choice we make, we shape our destiny, paving our way to a more liberated life.

It could be a decision we make, an action we take, a shift in perspective, or an attitude we adopt. Everything has an outcome. Every move has a result. Every moment matters.

Be deliberate about each choice along the way. Does the choice in front of you bring you closer to *you* and your goals? Does it keep you on your chosen path? Does it help you shape your vision?

Life is too short to squander potentially pivotal moments. Big or small, they all matter. In each moment you make a decision about your future. It may sound overstated, but it's true.

Respect the power of the now. It's your future.

Those who make the worst use of their time
are the first to complain of its shortness.
—Jean de La Bruyère

DAY 364
LOOK FOR LITTLE FREEDOMS

Personal freedom is a pretty immense concept. It's quite an ambition. But try not to be intimidated by the idea of it. Personal freedom doesn't have to be big and bold. You can have moments of sweet freedom each and every day.

Personal freedom is about breaking free. And we can break free in all sorts of ways. Each and every liberated moment is significant. Each one is worthwhile.

What's more: one liberated moment produces another. The more you taste personal freedom, the more of it you will create for yourself.

Look for those little freedoms. They're bigger than you think.

Freedom is nothing else but a chance to be better.
—Albert Camus

DAY 365
FREE YOURSELF

Today is a new day.

No more postponing your own growth. No more putting off your dreams. No more dangling your own carrot, keeping your personal vision just out of reach. You've stepped into the world of personal freedom. You've reclaimed passion, purpose, and potential. You've rediscovered yourself.

No longer delaying your own happiness, you're now growing your own dreams. One step at a time—and no step is too small—your path is becoming illuminated.

You've learned that any day is a good day to come to your own assistance. Any moment is a good moment to break out and break free.

Now the challenge is to continue the journey. It's to answer that daily call to action—the one that beckons you to an increasingly liberated life—and to take the next step in the direction of personal freedom.

Why not take that step today? Why not right now?

*Begin to free yourself at once by doing all that is possible
with the means you have, and as you proceed in this
spirit the way will open for you to do more.*
—George Clemenceau

You were born with potential.
You were born with goodness and trust.
You were born with ideals and dreams.
You were born with greatness.
You were born with wings.
You were not meant for crawling, so don't.
You have wings.
Learn to use them, and fly.
—Rumi

ABOUT THE AUTHOR

Kingsley Gallup, MA, LPC, NCC, DCC is a licensed professional counselor, nationally certified counselor, distance credentialed counselor, and certified mediator. She received her Bachelor of Arts from the University of Richmond and her Master of Arts in Counseling from Gordon-Conwell Theological Seminary. Kingsley lives in Kennebunk, Maine, with her husband, Les, and two children, Daisy and Zachary. Her current practice consists of private counseling, primarily in person and on the phone; public speaking; small groups; and workshops. Authentic living and her signature focus, personal freedom, are the driving themes behind Kingsley's work. Kingsley reminds her clients that as human beings we can indeed heal and transform—there is always hope for a new beginning.

Curiosity about the human condition and a passion for social service come naturally (or perhaps genetically) to Kingsley. Her grandfather, George H. Gallup, founded the Gallup Poll. Kingsley inherited a characteristic hunger that runs through the Gallup family—a hunger to know what people think and feel. She also inherited a deep commitment to meeting people precisely where they are and empowering and equipping them in that place.

Over the last fifteen years, Kingsley has served diverse populations, including incarcerated women, to whom she taught self-esteem and parenting classes; victims of natural disasters, with whom she did crisis intervention work; clients with HIV/AIDS, on whose behalf she helped run a wish-granting foundation; addicts and their loved ones, with whom she facilitated interventions; and clients of all ages seeking freedom from inauthentic living. Much of Kingsley's professional experience centers on The Meadows, a world-renowned residential treatment center for addictive and affective disorders in Wickenburg, Arizona, where she trained with some of her heroes in the field.

Her varied experiences and clientele continue to enrich her distinctive faith in human potential and in people's profound capacity for change.

**Discover more and contact Kingsley directly by visiting
The Gallup Institute for Personal Freedom at:
www.personalfreedominstitute.com.**